I0080187

Beyond Sunday

By
David Johnson

Copyright © 2025 by David Johnson

All rights reserved. No part of this publication may be reproduced, distributed, or transmitted in any form or by any means, including photocopying, recording, or other electronic or mechanical methods, without the prior written permission of the author, except in the case of brief quotations embodied in critical reviews and certain other noncommercial uses permitted by copyright law.

Published by Book Writing Pioneer
Cover design by Book Writing Pioneer
ISBN: Printed in the United States

BOOK WRITING
P I O N E E R

Table Of Contents

Praise For Beyond Sunday

As someone deeply committed to helping men reclaim their God-given identity through leadership, purpose, and community, *Beyond Sunday* felt like a prophetic charge wrapped in humility, truth, and grace. This book is not just a call to action—it's a mirror for every believer, especially the men who've been sitting on the sidelines, waiting for a sign. David's work *is* that sign.

What resonated most with me was the book's consistent heartbeat: *We were not saved to sit—we were saved to serve.* From the raw honesty of the introduction to the historical backdrop of grassroots faith movements, David masterfully bridges the gap between spiritual conviction and practical obedience. He doesn't shy away from naming what's broken—in the Church, in society, and within ourselves—but he also lights a path forward: *service rooted in love, guided by Christ, and done in community.*

For the men I walk with—the ones fighting to lead at home, in business, and in their own hearts—this book is deeply affirming. David's challenge to reject religious apathy and embrace gritty, street-level ministry mirrors what we teach: leadership begins when you take responsibility for what God has placed in front of you. Whether it's your family, your city, or your past, you don't need a title to start making a difference—you need a burden and a willingness to bleed for something bigger than yourself.

What I particularly love is that David doesn't write from a pedestal—he writes as a man in the trenches. His stories of men in recovery, real neighbors in need, and partnerships that defy religious gatekeeping give flesh to the kind of masculine Christianity our world is desperate for: one that protects, provides, and pursues people with the heart of Jesus.

Beyond Sunday is a book every man should read—not just to be inspired but to be *ignited.* It's a call back to servant-hearted masculinity, to be dangerous for good, and to carry the Gospel into the darkest corners of our communities—not with a megaphone, but with a towel and basin.

To David: Thank you for writing this. And to every man who reads it: don't just highlight the good parts—*go live them.*

Steve Baumgartner

CEO - Fire Forged Enterprises
Unlocking the Leader within, one man at a time

Evangelicals have not done a good job in recent years engaging the ills that plague American culture. From the carnage of the sexual revolution to the destruction brought about by the drug epidemic, the response of the American church has been less than stellar. In his book, Beyond Sunday, David Johnson gives both the biblical mandate and practical advice for how churches can re-engage our culture. Because many in the Evangelical church have chosen cultural disengagement, secular non-profits have filled the gap. With great insight, Johnson explains how the church can partner with these organizations to minister to the broken. Johnson also acknowledges the tension that is present when the church joins with secular non-profits and how these differences can be navigated without compromising the mission of the church. So, if you are looking for a "how-to" book written in a small group Bible study format that encourages you to get busy for the Kingdom, then I highly recommend "Beyond Sunday."

Marty Mclain

Author and Pastor

"Ambassador." This is just one of the great titles that God gives His followers in the Bible. Beyond Sunday offers an exemplary picture of how we, as Christians, are very specifically and intentionally called to live out this distinctive role. We are in a "strange land" representing a great God. Dave gets it and accurately assesses and empowers readers regarding our assignment. We are meant to impact this world, not just make our way through it in our own huddled groups. We are called to be Ambassadors of our faith and of our Father.

Beyond Sunday is a solid tool to help us fulfill the calling upon our lives. Please take the time to dive into this book and study how you, too, can be an Ambassador and have a larger impact in this world.

Ferrell Brown

Executive Director | Florida

Street Grace

Dedicated to my wife, Tammy

everything I am has

your fingerprints all over it.

Thank you for your love

And belief all these years

Thanks

Thanks go to my Heavenly Father before all else.

Without His love and forgiveness, I would be rudderless

And without purpose.

My wife Tammy for all the love for all these years, proofing my writing and adding just the right tone to make it perfect. Love you, baby!

To my dad for teaching me the value of helping others and how to be a man, father, and husband. Love ya, Pop.

To Chad, the one who made me a dad, Devon, my faithful sidekick and Bri, who has me wrapped around her finger, thanks for giving me the time to write this book, teach, and speak.

To Ben for opening my eyes to a world of service I had overlooked.

To Scott for the idea for this book even though he didn't know until it was too late.

To my Friday morning men: Chris B, Chris H, Justin, Josh, Jay, Rob, Ben, Bubba, Matt, Robert, Steve B, Tyler. Love you guys

To Ferrell and John D, loyal friends I don't deserve.

Foreword

I've walked through hell—addiction, war, loss, and the darkest corners of humanity. I've stared into the eyes of traffickers and seen children robbed of their innocence. I've buried friends who didn't make it out, and I've held the hands of survivors clawing their way back from the brink. That pain, that fire, became purpose. And from it was born *We Fight Monsters,* a frontline mission to take back what the darkness tried to claim—our streets, our homes, and our people.

So when my brother asked me to write this foreword, I didn't hesitate—because this book isn't theory. It's testimony. It's a call to arms. It's about the rising wave of people who aren't waiting on permission, programs, or pulpits. It's about men and women who hear the brokenness of this world like a war drum and run toward the sound.

I've seen what happens when the Church gets stuck in the sanctuary and forgets the streets. But I've also seen what happens when everyday people, whether fueled by faith, grief, or grit, step up and say, **Not on my block. Not on my watch.**

We've turned narco houses into sober living homes. We've taken trafficked children and given them therapy dogs and safety. We've housed mothers who got clean, found Christ, and reclaimed their babies from the system. And we've done it with little more than faith, fire, and people who still believe love is a verb.

This book will challenge you. It'll make you uncomfortable. Good. Because if your faith isn't moving your feet, it's time to wake up.

The Gospel doesn't just belong in stained glass windows. It belongs in the trenches—with the addicts, the trafficked, the lost, and left behind. Jesus didn't avoid the gutter. He walked straight into it. If we claim to follow Him, we better start doing the same.

So ask yourself: What breaks your heart? What's the holy discontent that keeps you up at night? That's the battlefield God's calling you to.

Let this book light a fire under your faith. And then, as we say in the field—let's go.

—Ben Owen, Founder, We Fight Monsters

Introduction

A while back, I was discussing with a close friend the state of the world and lamenting that no one seems to care that we are hurtling towards a future that none of us will recognize. My friend, Ben Owen, leads a couple of nonprofits that are attempting to take back the streets of my hometown, Memphis, TN. The struggle he has each day to raise enough money to stay relevant in his quest is daunting. Everyone wants to complain, but no one wants to step up and actually do the hard thing.

Ben mentioned a quote from retired Lt. Col. Scott Mann that said, *"It's up to us, no one is coming to save us,"* and that hit a nerve within me. I realized that he was right; our government is so broken that even if they have a program for it, the chances that it would actually help are minimal. Then, it hit me that the same could be said for our faith communities around the country.

Ben also told me that Scott talked about how a grassroots movement around the turn of the century had filled the gap left by churches and the government, and he felt like it was happening again with nonprofits like his. He described other groups that were doing great things as well; some were niche programs with a specific need, like covering old tattoos that represented ownership by another person, while others were broader, reaching the addicted, veterans, or displaced people in our communities.

I began listening and learning about all these diverse groups of people who felt called to help others. Some were driven by faith, others by their past, and some were driven by the sorrow of lost loved ones. Some were antagonistic toward organized religion, while others embraced it. But the common denominator was a calling to help their fellow man.

As of 2023, the U.S. nonprofit sector comprises approximately 1.8 million organizations, generating an estimated $3.7 trillion in annual revenue. Although this seems like a staggering amount, many of these organizations are global, sending the vast majority of their funds overseas. Graft and fraud further dilute the amount. According to a global study by the Association of Certified Fraud Examiners (ACFE), organizations, on average, lose about 5% of their annual revenue to fraud. Applying this percentage to the U.S. nonprofit sector suggests potential losses of up to $185 billion annually due to fraud.

In his book, "Nobody is Coming to Save You," Scott Mann talks about what he calls "communities of Practice." He says, *They are composed of diverse members from different backgrounds who share a common purpose in an ecosystem focused on solving a wicked, ill-structured problem.* All through the Bible, God used unbelievers to accomplish His will, yet we often refuse to bring all assets to bear on problems because we may not be completely aligned in our faiths. In a world that is so divided, we must find common ground to save the body so that we can allow God to save the soul. Or, as Scott says it, "Connect like our lives depended on it."

Since that time, I have listened to Scott talk about this very subject on podcasts and TV, and I had the opportunity to attend his play "Last Out" in New York. I began to be ashamed of my own failures to help others, to drive by, expecting the next car to stop. I read "Pineapple Express" (the story of how regular citizens filled the breach and got allies out of Afghanistan before it fell) and saw what true concern for your fellow man can look like. Then I began looking at the history and where we are today in Philanthropy and nonprofits, and this book quickly became a thing between Ben and me.

I hope it challenges you, makes you angry, and opens your eyes to how we, not God, are failing our world. The love of Christ, His redemptive work on the cross and the ultimate defeat of death are still the only answer to our world's ills.

All through the Bible, we see believers who failed to either do God's leading or failed to wait on His promise. Adam disobeyed God and ate from the wrong tree; Sarah gave her handmaiden, Hagar, to Abraham, her husband, to create heirs even though God had promised her an heir. Moses struck the rock in anger when God told him to speak to it. The nation of Israel demanded an earthly King instead of accepting God as their King.

Failing to listen and follow God has, time after time, had catastrophic effects on our world. From the fall of Eden to the Middle East conflict we still see today, the pattern is clear. Moses was denied entry into the promised land for disobeying God and the constant troubles Israel had with their leaders after they refused to accept God as their king. The evidence is everywhere—when people turn away from God, trouble follows. We need to heed God's calling, walk through the open doors, and partner with secular organizations that have the relationships and reach that we need to do good work for the Kingdom. Stop judging others who have not come to Christ and live a life that will make them want to. It's time to stand up and stand out in a world that desperately needs our help, needs a light and a direction that Christ can give. But we will never reach the least of these until we meet their basic needs, where they are, with no judgement and with the tools that God has provided.

But we are not living nor demonstrating that love to the world around us. We come across as aloof and unbending in our quest to reach the lost. Understand that I am not asking for a compromise of beliefs; the Bible speaks in black and white on many subjects, and we must stand upon His truths. But getting bogged down in personal convictions and decisions that keep us from partnering with others is wrong.

I lead a weekly men's group that is comprised of both seasoned Christian men and new Christians who are removed from the street by months, not years. I joke that I get very few amens, but I get a lot of Hell yeahs'. I am not offended because when these men pray, it is with a fervent faith that I am amazed by. These men challenge me as they fight addictions and problems that are so much harder than anything most of us see. The inhumanity they have lived through, and God has brought them out of, astounds me. All these men were brought out of that life and helped along their recovery by people who are not your typical Christ followers, but nevertheless, God has used them for great things—Men who would never listen to me but hear an authentic voice in Ben Owen and others like him.

I hope this book challenges you to fix that and to find your place to serve. At the end of the book, please look at those people and organizations that are doing good, some in God's name and some in response to their own pain and need to help others. Follow God's leading and find a cause to come alongside and be the hands and feet of Jesus. Go find our neighbors and love them.

Ground-up Grass Roots
Love Thy Neighbor is NOT a Metaphor

In the late 1800s and early 1900s, there was an influx of grassroots organizations that stepped up to do what the Government wasn't doing or wasn't willing to do. People took the initiative to meet the needs they saw going unanswered in society—answering social inequity, racial inequality, addiction and disaster relief, to name a few. The impact these organizations had on our nation changed the way we looked at our responsibilities to others and changed generations for the better.

In this section of the book, you will find a list of some of these, the impact each had on society, and the contributions they made to our world. The people who made the sacrifice when they saw a need and met that need head-on have left a legacy that changed our world.

In today's fast-paced, fully accessible world, it is much easier to see the inequity in our society by just logging on to the internet—Instant pictures of war, disasters, and human suffering all over the world at your fingertips. But oftentimes, the media decides what leads the story on the nightly news with the "if it bleeds, it leads" mentality. This approach skews the real stories behind hidden agendas, refusing to cover others who do not agree with their worldview.

Political differences freeze progress, and pressing issues languish in committee while politicians with big egos, ulterior motives, and backroom offers grandstand and argue for show. Woke ideologies, cancel-culture, and strident voices put our communities at odds. Secret funding and paid protests skew the real views that are held by the people, warping our values to bend to an ideology that is diametrically opposed to what our founding fathers intended.

The vast fissures in our society now leave great swaths of underserved people as our officials play politics, the church is scared to stand, and our people are more disconnected and apathetic.

But just like at the turn of the last century, there is a grassroots movement that is stirring among ordinary people. A grassroots movement is taking shape—one that bridges the gap between secular groups who see a need and concerned believers who feel the Holy Spirit calling them to action. Whether it is addiction, child protection, sex trafficking, veteran concerns, homelessness, or any number of other causes, God is moving in the hearts of average people to make a difference. On his podcast, Bill Courtney calls this an Army of Normal Folks.

Let's look at the impact the movement at the turn of the last century had on our country.

Alcoholics Anonymous (AA):

- **Founding:** Alcoholics Anonymous was founded in 1935 by Bill Wilson and Dr. Bob Smith, both of whom struggled with alcoholism themselves. The organization's primary purpose was to provide support and fellowship for individuals recovering from alcohol addiction. AA introduced the concept of a 12-step program, which became a cornerstone of addiction recovery worldwide.

- **Impact:** According to AA's own estimates, there are over 115,000 AA groups worldwide, with more than 2 million members. The organization's influence extends beyond its membership, as many addiction treatment programs incorporate AA's principles into their approaches to recovery.

Boy Scouts of America (BSA):

- **Founding:** Founded in 1910 by Sir Robert Baden-Powell and American businessman William D. Boyce, the Boy Scouts of America aimed to instill character, citizenship, and leadership skills in young boys. BSA introduced outdoor education, community service, and merit badge programs to promote personal development and civic engagement among youth.

- **Impact:** The organization has influenced millions of young Americans, fostering leadership, self-reliance, and service to others. Today, the Boy Scouts of America continues to provide valuable opportunities for character-building and leadership development through its scouting programs.

American Red Cross:

- **Founding:** Established in 1881 by Clara Barton, the American Red Cross is a humanitarian organization dedicated to providing disaster relief, blood donations, health and safety training, and support to military families.

- **Impact:** The American Red Cross has had a profound impact on American society by saving lives, alleviating suffering, and promoting public health and safety. Its volunteers and staff continue to provide critical assistance and support to individuals and communities facing adversity.

National Association for the Advancement of Colored People (NAACP):

- **Founding:** Founded in 1909 by a group of activists, including W.E.B. Du Bois, Mary White Ovington, and Ida B. Wells, the NAACP is the nation's oldest and largest civil rights organization.

- **Impact:** The NAACP's advocacy and activism have led to significant advancements in civil rights legislation, including the desegregation of schools, voting rights protections, and anti-discrimination laws. The organization continues to work toward its mission of achieving racial equality and social justice for all Americans.

United Way (1887):

- **Founding:** In Denver, Colorado, 1887, religious leaders founded the Charity Organization Society, the first United Way organization that planned and coordinated local services and conducted a single fundraising campaign for 22 agencies. The first fundraising campaign raised $21,700.

- **Impact:** United Way has mobilized resources, volunteers, and expertise to address pressing social needs and create lasting change in communities across the country. It has provided vital support to individuals and families facing economic hardship, educational barriers, and health disparities.

Salvation Army (1865):

- **Founding:** The Salvation Army was founded in 1865 as the "East London Christian Mission" in London by one-time Methodist preacher William Booth and his wife Catherine. It can trace its origins to the Blind Beggar Tavern. In 1878, Booth reorganized the mission, becoming its first general, and introduced the military structure, which has been retained as a matter of tradition. The Salvation Army's highest priority is its Christian principles.

- **Impact:** The Salvation Army has offered compassionate care and practical assistance to millions of individuals and families experiencing poverty, homelessness, addiction, and crisis. It has provided hope and support to the most vulnerable members of society.

Habitat for Humanity (1976, but rooted in 1942):

- **Mission:** Habitat for Humanity works to eliminate substandard housing and homelessness by building and renovating affordable homes, advocating for affordable housing policies, and mobilizing volunteers and resources.

- **Impact:** Habitat for Humanity has helped millions of families achieve homeownership, stability, and self-reliance. It has revitalized communities, strengthened neighborhoods, and promoted dignity and opportunity for all.

Lions Clubs International:

- **Founding (1917):** Lions Clubs International was founded in 1917 by Melvin Jones, a Chicago businessman, with the aim of bringing together community-minded individuals to address pressing social and humanitarian needs.

- **Impact:**

   Vision and Hearing Care: Lions Clubs International's vision and hearing programs have improved the quality of life for millions of individuals with visual and hearing impairments.

   Disaster Response: Lions Clubs International's rapid response to disasters has provided critical assistance to communities in times of crisis.

   Youth Empowerment: Empowered countless young people to become leaders in their communities, make positive contributions to society, and develop lifelong values of service and philanthropy.

In all these organizations, faith, concern for inequity, or the needs of their fellow man drove groups of individuals to start life-impacting ministries that changed the culture and fiber of our land. Today, not only are they still around, but they thrive, still making a difference. Alcoholics Anonymous still reaches an estimated 2 million members, while the Salvation Army is assisting approximately 23 million Americans annually. But this is still woefully inadequate.

Although in today's world, we aren't dealing with Jim Crow, starvation, and lack of health care the way our grandparents were in 1900, we are still being dealt very serious social blows. Just look to the streets of our biggest cities where homelessness is rampant, drug addiction is killing our young people, and sexual abuse of women and children runs rampant. Pornography is impacting our children, stealing their childhood long before it naturally should. Methamphetamine, Fentanyl, and contaminated drugs are killing a whole generation, and our borders leak like a sieve, allowing unfettered access to our children.

Sex Trafficking

Prevalence in the United States: In 2024, an estimated 24,000 individuals were victims of human trafficking within the U.S.

Demographics: Approximately 75% of these victims were female, and about 40% were minors, indicating a significant impact on women and children.

Global Trends: The United Nations Office on Drugs and Crime reported a 25% increase in detected trafficking victims globally between 2019 and 2022, with children comprising 38% of these victims.

Child Sexual Exploitation

Online Exploitation Reports: In 2023, the National Center for Missing & Exploited Children's CyberTipline received over 36.2

million reports of suspected child sexual exploitation, a 12% increase from the previous year.

AI-Generated Exploitative Material: The rise of AI technology has led to an increase in AI-generated child sexual abuse material (CSAM). A global survey indicated that 50% of law enforcement officers encountered AI-generated CSAM in 2024.

Youth Exposure to Nonconsensual Imagery: A 2023 report revealed that 7% of minors had reshared someone else's sexual images, and nearly 20% had seen nonconsensually reshared intimate images of others.

Negative Impacts of Pornography

Early Exposure: Studies indicate that the average age of first exposure to pornography is around 12 years old, often occurring accidentally.

Psychological and Behavioral Effects: Early exposure to pornography can distort sexual development, leading to unrealistic sexual standards and desensitization to violence.

Legislative Responses: In response to these concerns, several U.S. states have enacted legislation requiring age verification for accessing online sexual content to protect minors from exposure.

The Drug and Alcohol Epidemic

Overdose Fatalities: In the year ending June 30, 2024, the U.S. experienced approximately 97,000 drug overdose deaths

Opioid Involvement: Opioids, particularly synthetic variants like Fentanyl, continue to be a major contributor to overdose deaths. In 2021, synthetic opioids were involved in approximately 71,000 of the over 106,000 drug overdose deaths reported.

Underage Substance Use and Exposure

Alcohol Consumption: In 2024, 42% of 12th graders reported consuming alcohol in the past year. Among 10th graders, it was 26%, and among 8th graders, it was 13%.

Illicit Drug Use: The Monitoring the Future Survey indicates substance use among adolescents in 2024—3.4% of 8th graders reported using illicit drugs other than marijuana in the past 12 months, and rates for 10th and 12th graders were 4.4% and 6.5%, respectively.

Nicotine Pouch Usage: Despite overall declines in substance use, the use of nicotine pouches among 12th graders has increased, rising from 3% in 2023 to 6% in 2024.

Marijuana Use: In 2023, 4% of 12th-grade students reported using prescription medications in the past year.

Crime goes unpunished, and the incarcerated go unrehabilitated, creating a cycle that is never-ending and killing our inner cities. Fatherless children clog our systems as welfare steals the dignity of our poor. The systems built to help are broken and contaminated with bureaucratic slugs that fail to even attempt to do their jobs.

But on the horizon, there is a ray of hope as we begin to see survivors returning to help those caught in the webs they themselves escaped. Family members, in memory of their loved ones, are beginning charities and movements to protect the families of others whom they don't even know.

From veterans' organizations to trafficking and abuse of fatherless children, prison reform, and judicial reform, there are so many other niche opportunities to help others that it staggers the imagination. These volunteers are stepping up and doing the basic tenet that Jesus gave us: to love our neighbor as ourselves.

All across the landscape, these survivors are banding together, supporting each other, and standing unified in the gap for our country and our world. With little support, these patriots and Christians are doing it in spite of, not because of. Following the leading of the Holy Spirit, these Christ followers are doing the work that our churches and our leaders refuse to do. Going where Jesus spent his time—the streets and gutters of our cities—these heroes are making a difference in lives all over our country. In many instances, these are brand-new believers with the passion and drive to bring others along with them.

This begs the question: Where are the bulk of believers? Where is the church in reaching out to the hurting in our communities? Our buildings are full; mega-churches preach that we can have our best life now. Yet Jesus told us they will hate you because they first hated me. (John 15:18; Mark 13:13; Luke 21:17) We need less religion and more Christ. If Jesus were here today, He would be flipping more than just tables.

Where is our passion for the lost? Do we truly understand what Jesus called us to do? In the next section, we will delve into what Jesus called the 2nd commandment, one that everything in our faith hinges on: "to love your neighbor as yourself."

So, the next time you say to yourself, "Why doesn't somebody do something about that?" Don't look outward; look at yourself. Say to yourself, "What can I do about that?" Ask God what He would have you do, and then do it. And then act! Look around you, find a purpose, and serve.

If not you, who?

If not now, when?

Let's go.

Chapter 1

Missing the Mark
The Church

---⌒◉⌒---

The church has been a force for good and, in some cases, for evil throughout history, if we are talking about the church as a system. The crusades, the witch hunts, and other persecutions perpetrated by leaders claiming Christian authority over people and regions have done more to damage the office of the church than any outside pressure or authority. On the other hand, without the church and its people, there would be far more poverty and hurt all over the world. When the church is within God's will and following the teachings of our Savior, Jesus Christ, there is not a more powerful, dedicated group of humans on the planet.

But therein lies the biggest issue the church has: we are all human and, according to the Bible, born with a corrupt nature. Although we are redeemed through the sacrifice of Jesus, His death, burial, and resurrection offered us redemption, not perfection. The sin nature in this world is all-encompassing and permeates everything around us. We struggle every day with temptations and desires that are diametrically opposed to our faith in Christ and what we are called to be, and it will not change until we are in the presence of our Father in heaven.

1

The Universality of Sin

There is no one without sin. Since Adam fell to sin in the Garden of Eden, a sin nature has been passed to every person born into this fallen world.

- **Romans 3:23:** "For all have sinned and fall short of the glory of God."

- **Romans 5:12:** "Therefore, just as sin came into the world through one man, and death through sin, and so death spread to all men because all sinned."

- **Psalm 14:2-3:** "The Lord looks down from heaven on the children of man, to see if there are any who understand, who seek after God. They have all turned aside; together they have become corrupt; there is none who does good, not even one."

Inherited Sin Nature

It is inherited, a part of us that we fight daily. Although when we accept Christ, we are a new creature, we do not lose this sin nature, and this is the reason Jesus had to pay our debt on the cross once and for all. We cannot face a righteous God but through the blood of Christ.

- **Psalm 51:5:** "Behold, I was brought forth in iniquity, and in sin did my mother conceive me."

- **Ephesians 2:3:** "Among whom we all once lived in the passions of our flesh, carrying out the desires of the body and the mind, and were by nature children of wrath, like the rest of mankind."

The Struggle with Sin

Paul speaks of the destructiveness of our nature and the struggle that we have with our old selves. Our old flesh, still steeped in sin, battles against a new heart but one that is still tarnished by this world.

- **Romans 7:18-20:** "For I know that nothing good dwells in me, that is, in my flesh. For I have the desire to do what is right, but not the ability to carry it out. For I do not do the good I want, but the evil I do not want is what I keep on doing. Now if I do what I do not want, it is no longer I who do it, but sin that dwells within me."

- **Galatians 5:17:** "For the desires of the flesh are against the Spirit, and the desires of the Spirit are against the flesh, for these are opposed to each other, to keep you from doing the things you want to do."

Holy Discontent

When I speak of the church missing the mark, I don't speak of our sanctuaries, our denominations, or our congregations. I am speaking of the church body, which is each of us individually. We are called. Individually, we are called. The purpose of this book is to get the people of God to get up off our collective backsides and serve our savior. We were not called to a pew on Sunday; we were called to serve. Yet Sunday morning is filled with just-in-time worshippers who sit in a cushioned seat, sing 5 or 6 songs, listen to a sermon that may or may not include the name of Jesus, listen to a

3

prayer, stand through an altar call, maybe, and go home without ever talking to anyone.

What if your fingers did not communicate with each other through your nervous system? Your hands would be useless, unable to feed yourself, write a letter, or even point out something of interest. God compares us to the human body. Just as the human body has different parts, each with its own function, God has given each of us unique talents to serve His purpose. What is your church failing to do because you aren't using your talents? Who is not being reached for Christ because you are failing to show up? What will you say to God when you stand before Him, and all the things that could have been are brought forward? How will you explain you were just too busy to show up?

Let's have a real conversation about how we can be better used by God and how we can step up and serve our fellow man within and outside the church. Recognize where God is working, step up to the plate, and do something that could change someone else's world and eternity. Jesus met the earthly needs before he attacked the heart's needs. When he talked to the woman at the well, he dealt with her shame, not her sin; he showed a compassion she had not known and, in doing so, opened her eyes to a Living Water. Who is God calling you to meet, where is He calling you to use your talents, and what job has God laid on your heart to do? Let's find out.

Becoming a Neighbor

What is a neighbor? Its old English predecessor meant near dweller, or someone who lives more near. We look around and see the houses on our street, in our community, our city, our county, our state, and our world, and realize that we know almost no one. How do we love our neighbors when we don't even know them?

We lived closed lives, tight circles of acquaintances with very few true connections with others that go beyond pleasantries and superficial interactions—Lives that don't intersect with those who need us or produce opportunities to help others. Living lonely lives of desperation that are unfulfilled and miss the mark that our savior called us to.

Further, we segregate ourselves into homogenous enclaves of like-minded individuals from the same social and ethnic backgrounds who look like us and don't challenge our view of who we are. We fail to reach out to others who look different, worship differently, and make us uncomfortable. We remain safe in our self-made bubble of isolation and distance, keeping our false views of our work and accomplishments for the kingdom safe from reality.

We choose comfort over compassion, focusing on full pews instead of busy streets. We forget that the Gospel is a verb, not a brand. In today's society, we need less "religion" and more Christ. We need to stop asking WWJD because we already know! Despite having the right theology, we are still missing the Gospel.

We need to become Holy Troublemakers, making waves, challenging the status quo, and turning over tables. OUR FAITH NEEDS TO HIT LIKE A THUNDERCLAP AND SPARK LIKE A MOVEMENT!

Sunday morning church checks our box of service, self-congratulations for our service to a God who doesn't recognize our offerings because they don't even rise above the ceiling. We walk past the hurting, needy, and dying to get to a sanctuary with other believers who fail to follow the most basic command of our Lord: to love like He did. He told us to love our neighbors as ourselves, and we don't even know them.

We spend our time preaching Love but practicing apathy!

We are missing the mark!

When Jesus was asked in Luke 10: 25-37 how to receive eternal life, he responded like he often did with a parable:

25 And behold, a certain [a]lawyer stood up and tested Him, saying, "Teacher, what shall I do to inherit eternal life?"

26 He said to him, "What is written in the law? What is your reading *of it?*"

27 So he answered and said, "'You shall love the Lord your God with all your heart, with all your soul, with all your strength, and with all your mind,' and 'your neighbor as yourself.'"

[28] And He said to him, "You have answered rightly; do this and you will live."

[29] But he, wanting to justify himself, said to Jesus, "And who is my neighbor?"

[30] Then Jesus answered and said: "A certain *man* went down from Jerusalem to Jericho, and fell among [b]thieves, who stripped him of his clothing, wounded *him,* and departed, leaving *him* half dead. [31] Now by chance a certain priest came down that road. And when he saw him, he passed by on the other side. [32] Likewise a Levite, when he arrived at the place, came and looked, and passed by on the other side. [33] But a certain Samaritan, as he journeyed, came where he was. And when he saw him, he had compassion. [34] So he went to *him* and bandaged his wounds, pouring on oil and wine; and he set him on his own animal, brought him to an inn, and took care of him. [35] On the next day, [c]when he departed, he took out two denarii, gave *them* to the innkeeper, and said to him, 'Take care of him; and whatever more you spend, when I come again, I will repay you.' [36] So which of these three do you think was neighbor to him who fell among the thieves?"

[37] And he said, "He who showed mercy on him."

Then Jesus said to him, "Go and do likewise."

Pretty self-explanatory, but let's look at a few things:

Jesus singled out the position of the first two travelers who passed by, the priest and the Levite. Although we don't know the exact reason Jesus used a priest in the story, we can rest assured he was Jewish and part of the religious elite and, therefore, should have had compassion for a hurting person. But probably because he did not want to be inconvenienced if the man was dead or had died, he just passed by.

Because if a priest became unclean by touching a dead body, he would have to undergo a rigorous ritual cleansing for over 7 days. (Numbers 19:2-13 and Ezekiel 44:24-27) This would have, by all accounts, been a great inconvenience for the priest and the temple. Perhaps this is the reason the Priest failed to stop. Regardless, it showed a lack of compassion for his fellow man.

The Levite, although not listed as a priest, would have probably been well versed in the law. At least he crossed the road and made sure it wasn't someone he knew or a fellow temple member. But he, too cruised on by without giving help or even sending help back.

But then, amazingly enough, a traveler who was considered heretical by Jewish society, a Samaritan, feels compassion and cares for the hurting. Samaritans were considered beneath the Jews and treated with great disdain, much like "devout" Christians can begin to forget who they were before Christ saved them and look down on those who are struggling or have not believed. Jesus knew that to admonish the spiritual leaders and recognize the Samaritan as the true neighbor would infuriate the Jews he was talking to.

A risky thing to do when you are already on the radar of the religious elite. But Jesus was making a point. There are many who follow the teachings of God but get caught up in the minutia of laws, rules, appearances and inconvenience. The same priest was already walking miles to go serve at the temple but could not be bothered to help a dying man.

The Samaritan not only dressed his wounds, put him on his donkey, and spent his money to get him whole, but he also promised to return and pay any overages that were not covered by his money already. This is the picture of God's love that Jesus brought us—A living example of a servant's heart to his neighbor.

Reflections

What have you done when confronted with a person in need? Did you stop to help? Did you hope someone else would stop? Looking back, what would Christ have had you do?

_____

_____

_____

Have you ever excused not helping someone because of time, danger, or inconvenience? When reflecting on the cross, how much weight should inconvenience or time play in loving your neighbor?

_____

_____

_____

When you think of service, what comes to mind? Is it a process of loving your neighbor?

_____

_____

_____

Who makes you uncomfortable? Why?

_____

_____

_____

What gifts do you have that others need?

_____

_____

_____

Where is a place to serve in your neighborhood?

_____

_____

_____

What are you doing to make this world a better place?

_____

_____

_____

Are you accepting of people outside your circle of belief coming alongside to help?

_____

_____

_____

Who in your neighborhood can you provide a needed service to?

_____

_____

_____

What local charity can you help with?

_____

_____

_____

If your neighbors needed help, would they feel comfortable knocking on your door?

_____

_____

_____

Are you approachable? Available? Willing?

_____

_____

_____

What will you do in the next week to show love to your neighbor?

_____

_____

_____

Prayer for guidance-

Heavenly Father, You have given us a perfect road map to living a life that is filled with love for You and love for our neighbor. Help us to love with a love like Yours. Burden our hearts for the lost and hurting in our world and show us how we can serve our neighbor and show them the way to eternal life. Forgive us for our sense of piety, remind us of who we were before You saved us, and keep us humble and open to Your leadership. Amen

David Johnson

Chapter 2

Who is my Neighbor?

———⟲◉⟳———

Mr. Rogers sang every day about being neighbors. His calm voice and ability to connect with the smallest of us made us want to be part of his neighborhood. He set milestones and broke barriers as he taught the least of us to accept everyone and love our neighbor. Mr. Rogers once said, "If you could only sense how important you are to the lives of those you meet, how important you can be to the people you may never even dream of. There is something of yourself that you leave at every meeting with another person." It was a different time when a kind father singing a song captured our attention and made us want to be good neighbors.

He also knew that sometimes just doing something is enough, "Some days, doing 'the best we can' may still fall short of what we would like to be able to do, but life isn't perfect on any front—and doing what we can with what we have is the most we should expect of ourselves or anyone else." Being present, paying attention, and noticing are so important in our disconnected society.

In today's world, we have become more disconnected from society, living life in reels, posts, views and likes. We rely on virtual relationships, seek opinions from influencers, and measure our self-worth by the number of likes our cat pictures get on Facebook. Too many in today's world have little to no relational interactions on a daily basis, relying on social media to fuel most, if not all, of their interactions. A recent study by Cigna found that 61% of Americans report feeling lonely. Highlighting the need for us to reach out to our neighbors, build bridges, and create a community of support.

A few months back, I noticed a group of middle school kids at a bus stop. There were probably six kids standing within a 20-foot radius, all standing alone, all on their phones, all oblivious to anything else around them. I contrasted this to the way I remembered bus stops and rides in grade school and wondered what their future relationships with others would be like. They were wasting the formative years of learning how to interact with others, build relationships, and forge friendships. According to an October 2023 Pew Research poll, 8% of Americans have no close friends. Is there any wonder we have an epidemic of suicide and drug abuse?

Are we becoming a society filled with relationally challenged people who cannot relate or connect with our neighbors? According to the 2023 Surgeon General's Advisory, from 2003 to 2023, the average time Americans spent alone increased by approximately 24 hours per month, while time spent socializing in person decreased by about 20 hours monthly. Do we even know who our neighbors are? On your street, how many homes are you familiar with? How many families?

We drive down the streets in our neighborhoods, and no one is outside. We don't visit at the mailbox; kids aren't riding their bikes, and in-home visits are nearly non-existent. We don't know our neighbors right next door, much less the wider definition that Jesus used as he told us to love our neighbor as ourselves. So, what is Jesus calling us to?

In Mark 12, Jesus is asked what the greatest commandment is, and His response is all about love. **[29] Jesus answered him, "The [k]first of all the commandments *is:* 'Hear, O Israel, the Lord our God, the Lord is one. [30] And you shall love the Lord your God with all your heart, with all your soul, with all your mind, and with all your strength.' [l]This *is* the first commandment. [31] And the second, like *it, is* this: 'You shall love your neighbor as yourself.' There is no other commandment greater than these."**

Love in Motion

What does that love look like? If we compare God's love for us to our love for our neighbor, we will come far short of the mark. But if we strive to put the interest of others above ours, make sure their basic needs are met when we can, and strive to lead them to the Lord, then we have fulfilled the basic calling Jesus gave us.

Love is evident in every aspect of our faith. The Ten Commandments are broken into Love of God and Love of Man. The first 5 commandments are about loving GOD, and the second 5 are all about loving our fellow man and doing him no harm. It makes living a spirit-filled life seem easy, but achieving that level of "putting others above yourself" is daunting when you realize that man is fallen and, therefore, full of sin, selfishness, and ego that makes getting along harder than it needs to be.

Love of God and love of our neighbor are at the very center of our faith. No other religion was founded on Love like Christianity. From John 3:16, **"For God so loved the world that He gave His only begotten Son, that whosoever believes in Him should not perish but have everlasting life."** To Romans 5: 8-11: **⁸ But God demonstrates His own love toward us, in that while we were still sinners, Christ died for us. ⁹ Much more then, having now been justified by His blood, we shall be saved from wrath through Him. ¹⁰ For if when we were enemies we were reconciled to God through the death of His Son, much more, having been reconciled, we shall be saved by His life. ¹¹ And not only *that,* but we also rejoice in God through our Lord Jesus Christ, through whom we have now received the reconciliation.**

We see that God loved us in spite of who we were, so much so that he sent His Son to die a horrible death on the cross. We have no other context for this level of love. The closest we see in this world is the parent-child relationship, as most parents would lay their lives down for their children. So, it makes perfect sense that we refer to God as our father. But realizing the depth of the distance between who God is and who we are would be more likened to the relationship between ourselves and an ant farm. For the perfection of God and the depraved heart of man do not even belong in the same universe, yet God sent His only son as the propitiation for our sin—the perfect sacrifice that covered ALL our sins, past, present, and future.

So, who are we to say who is lovable, who is beyond help, or who is worthy to be saved? The Bible says, "All have sinned," and we have "all fallen short." Without the blood of Christ covering our sins, there is not a person on this earth who can stand before God without being obliterated by the purity and magnificence of the maker of this universe. God had to hide Moses in the cleft of the rock and allow him to see His fleeting back because any more would have killed him.

We have no right to judge the lost and hurting in this world, as we would still be in our sin if the Holy Spirit had not pricked our hearts and called us to Himself. Grace came down and covered our depravity; we are no better than just forgiven. The lost are in denial and still living without Christ and left to their own devices; they will die in their sin. But if we allow God to use us, to show the lost that the shed blood of Christ Jesus on the cross makes a difference, fills a void, and answers every question, then we are doing what God called us to do.

Being given an unconditional pardon for the sins that we have committed should awaken in us a desire to repay the debt that was forgiven. By spreading the Gospel with our neighbors, we begin to share the free gift that was offered to us. But every day, many of us walk by burning buildings filled with sleeping families, refusing to bang on the door and warn them of the imminent danger, letting them burn in an everlasting fire that will not be quenched. We stand guilty before God and our fellow man for refusing to tell them about the good news of Jesus Christ. It is time to wake up and realize that the time to harvest is getting short, the return of Jesus Christ is imminent, and our neighbors are asleep in their beds, unaware.

But who are our neighbors? Where are we supposed to start when obeying God's edict to Love our Neighbor? Although Jesus gives no specific range or territory, he does give us the command to "Go into all the world." But in Luke 24: 46-47, he goes a little deeper when he said to start in Jerusalem: **46 Then He said to them, "Thus it is written, [1]and thus it was necessary for the Christ to suffer and to rise from the dead the third day, 47 and that repentance and remission of sins should be preached in His name to all nations, beginning at Jerusalem.** So, it is most important that we start, but also that we do it close to home first. Start with your community, with the hurting, the ones who are hungry for an answer to the hurt in their heart. Love them with the love that God showed us. By demonstrating the love of Christ, meeting them where they are, addressing their needs, and accepting who they are currently outside of Christ, we show them the reason they should turn to faith in Jesus.

It is time to start. God commanded us, and we cannot be in His will until every day is given to an openness to be the feet, hands, and heart of Jesus in our broken world. Waiting for the church is not an option, we need to stop just singing worship songs and start living them. The world needs to see the Gospel working in unexpected places.

Reflections:

What keeps you from connecting to your community?

_____

_____

_____

What are you currently doing to lead others to Christ?

_____

_____

_____

Write down on paper the answer to the following 3 questions:

1. Why do I need to accept Jesus?
2. How do I get saved?
3. How do I know that God accepted my prayer?

_____

_____

_____

List 3 ways to volunteer your time in ways to show Jesus to others.

_____

_____

_____

Are you generous with your time, money, and talents?

_____

_____

_____

Prayer for guidance:

Heavenly Father, You have commanded Your children to spread the good news of the cross, and I want to obey Your call. Show me those that You would have me embrace with Your love and break my heart for their salvation. Put in me an unwavering desire to reach them by showing them You through the way I live my life. Give me the ability to meet their needs and come alongside them wherever they are. Give me the words at the appropriate time to lead them to You. Help me find places to volunteer with like-minded followers to increase my reach and effectiveness. Amen

David Johnson

Chapter 3

Where is the Church?

———∽●∾———

A building was never Jesus' idea for his church. The church has always been God's people, coming together to edify one another and spread the good news. Jesus told Peter it was upon him that he would build His church, and later, Peter led the service where the Holy Spirit descended and changed the trajectory of mankind.

There is an old saying, "If you ever find a perfect church, don't join it because you will ruin it." A funny but true statement because all of us are imperfect and subject to bad decisions, bad attitudes, and bad conduct. In my late teen years and early adulthood, I experienced two separate church upheavals that resulted in staff leaving and members changing churches. As a teenager, this marred my view of the church and made me cynical about the motives and power structures in churches. When, as a young adult with a young family, it happened in another church, Christians acting unchristian, it set my opinion in stone that churches are imperfect people, saved by grace, but still imperfect and prone to selfish acts that hurt each other.

In every verse, the church is referred to as a living thing, a body of believers, not a building or sanctuary to be met in. See below:

Now, when they had come and gathered the church together, they reported all that God had done with them, and that He had opened the door of faith to the Gentiles. Acts 14:27

So, the churches were strengthened in the faith and increased in number daily. Acts 16:5

Therefore, take heed to yourselves and to all the flock, among which the Holy Spirit has made you overseers, to shepherd the church of God which He purchased with His own blood. Acts 20:28

The church is a body of believers, a growing, living organism made up of those who believe in Jesus Christ and His resurrection, who have accepted His shed blood for the forgiveness of their sins and gather together for the edification of each other and the evangelism of the lost.

Jesus would not need a pulpit.

The churches' primary functions are Evangelism, Discipleship, and Church planting. How should each of these be viewed with respect to reaching our Neighbor?

Evangelism—every believer should be able to explain their faith, how they came to faith, and how others can receive the gift that that faith brings. Whether it is the Roman road or another system you feel comfortable with, there are certain mile markers that must be covered in order to walk someone to faith.

- Our need for salvation – Romans 3:22-26: **For there is no difference; [23] for all have sinned and fall short of the glory of**

God, [24] being justified [g]freely by His grace through the redemption that is in Christ Jesus, [25] whom God set forth *as* a [h]propitiation by His blood, through faith, to demonstrate His righteousness... In no uncertain terms, the Bible says that ALL have sinned, and only by the blood of Christ can we be redeemed. The propitiation, payment, was in the blood of the sinless lamb of God. The only way for the forgiveness of sin was the shedding of blood. The problem was that the sacrifices given could not cover future sins because they came from a world ravaged by sin. Only the shed blood of a perfect man could cover the sins of the whole world for eternity. Because Jesus was born to a virgin, he had no sin nature, and by living a sinless life, he qualified as our redemptive sacrifice. The acceptance of that sacrifice as your sin payment saves your soul and allows God to look on you as a sinless child of God, adopted into his forever family.

- Romans 10: 9-13 speaks of the need for confession of your sins, admitting that you know you are a sinner, that without the shed blood of Christ, there is no hope of salvation.

[9] that if you confess with your mouth the Lord Jesus and believe in your heart that God has raised Him from the dead, you will be saved. [10] For with the heart one believes unto righteousness, and with the mouth confession is made unto salvation. [11] For the Scripture says, "Whoever believes on Him will not be put to shame." [12] For there is no distinction between Jew and Greek, for the same Lord over all is rich to

all who call upon Him. [13] For "whoever calls on the name of the Lord shall be saved."

Without confession, there can be no payment because no debt has been acknowledged. When we acknowledge our sin debt coupled with a belief in the power of the shed blood of Jesus and a turning from those sins, we achieve the atoning power of the blood and are saved. Being redeemed, we are now the adopted children of God, never to be disowned, and qualified for all the blessings that come with being the child of the creator of this world and an everlasting life in heaven with Him.

As followers of Christ, we must all be ready to lead the lost to Jesus. This is the mission he has called us to. Although God does not need us to call others to Himself, He allows us to be used in that mission, and we should be honored that God entrusts us to serve Him. WE are all evangelists and need to be prepared to fulfill the role God has for us. It could be by prayer, giving, witnessing, preaching or going to the worst places in our world to help others. But we are all called to love, first and foremost, TO LOVE.

Discipleship – the edification of the saints is the next purpose of the church. The Bible talks about the Christ follower as a babe who moves from milk to meat as he matures in his faith. The biggest problem with many churchgoers is that they never get beyond milk. They never mature to the point of being useful to God. They believe that showing up on Sunday is enough and they are serving God, but the Bible teaches differently. Hebrews 5:12-14: **[12] For though by this time you ought to be teachers, you need *someone* to teach**

you again the first principles of the [b]**oracles of God; and you have come to need milk and not solid food.** [13] **For everyone who partakes** *only* **of milk** *is* **unskilled in the word of righteousness, for he is a babe.** [14] **But solid food belongs to those who are** [c]**of full age,** *that is,* **those who by reason of** [d]**use have their senses exercised to discern both good and evil.**

We are to concentrate on our growth in the knowledge and faith that will grow us into useful tools for the church. We are not called to be only babies in the faith but to grow and mature into evangelists and teachers in our own right, benefitting the family of God and reaching the world for Christ.

Church planting – as Jesus prepared to ascend to the right hand of the Father, he commanded us to go into all nations

[18] **And Jesus came and spoke to them, saying, "All authority has been given to Me in heaven and on earth.** [19] **Go** [c]**therefore and make disciples of all the nations, baptizing them in the name of the Father and of the Son and of the Holy Spirit,** [20] **teaching them to observe all things that I have commanded you; and lo, I am with you always,** *even* **to the end of the age."** [d]**Amen.** Matthew 28: 18-20 is our marching orders as Jesus leaves us behind to carry the Good News to a lost world. When this is coupled with the parable of the Nobleman's servants, it puts much more onus on our responsibility. Luke 19:12-27 says, **"A certain nobleman went into a far country to receive for himself a kingdom and to return.** [13] **So he called ten of his servants, delivered to them ten** [e]**minas, and said to them, 'Do business till I come.'** [14] **But**

his citizens hated him, and sent a delegation after him, saying, 'We will not have this *man* to reign over us.'

¹⁵ "And so it was that when he returned, having received the kingdom, he then commanded these servants, to whom he had given the money, to be called to him, that he might know how much every man had gained by trading. ¹⁶ Then came the first, saying, 'Master, your mina has earned ten minas.' ¹⁷ And he said to him, 'Well *done,* good servant; because you were faithful in a very little, have authority over ten cities.' ¹⁸ And the second came, saying, 'Master, your mina has earned five minas.' ¹⁹ Likewise he said to him, 'You also be over five cities.'

²⁰ "Then another came, saying, 'Master, here is your mina, which I have kept put away in a handkerchief. ²¹ For I feared you, because you are [f]an austere man. You collect what you did not deposit and reap what you did not sow.' ²² And he said to him, 'Out of your own mouth I will judge you, *you* wicked servant. You knew that I was an austere man, collecting what I did not deposit and reaping what I did not sow. ²³ Why then did you not put my money in the bank, that at my coming I might have collected it with interest?'

²⁴ "And he said to those who stood by, 'Take the mina from him, and give *it* to him who has ten minas.' ²⁵ (But they said to him, 'Master, he has ten minas.') ²⁶ 'For I say to you, that to everyone who has will be given; and from him who does not have, even what he has will be taken away from him. ²⁷ But bring

here those enemies of mine, who did not want me to reign over them, and slay *them* before me.'"

Jesus left us to work, and we will be held accountable for the work we do, the people we serve, and lead to Christ and discipleship. I truly believe that the most surprised people at the end will be churchgoers who are turned away because, as James says, "Faith without works is dead." If you do not feel a need to serve in some capacity for the Lord, there is either a deep division between you and the Father or there is a problem in your salvation. If we are not spreading the Gospel, planting new bodies of believers, and nurturing those babes in Christ, we will be held accountable.

I often envision a scene in Heaven as God is handing out the awards at the ***end of the world award ceremony***. God hands me my reward and then walks me over to a closet that says "Dave" on it. God says, "My child, this is what I had planned for you," as He opens the door. Behind that small closet door is a giant cavern filled with all sorts of treasures that God had intended to be mine. Lives I could have impacted, issues I could have been the solution to, souls I could have led to Christ, and blessings I could have been. Instead, I look in my hand at the award I had been proud of a few seconds earlier and realize what a failure my life had been. I look at God, and the sad look on His face tells me He understands my pain. "My child," He says," you were so busy in the world that you missed so much in the next. Your job, your selfishness, and your laziness cost you so much. But you are my child, and I love you. Go enjoy your reward." I walk away with tears in my eyes, knowing that I had failed my Father, still in heaven, but with little evidence that I loved my Lord and far less reward than I could have had.

Matthew 25 puts this into perspective from Jesus himself: **[c]**

[c] **"When the Son of Man comes in His glory, and all the [c]holy angels with Him, then He will sit on the throne of His glory. [c] All the nations will be gathered before Him, and He will separate them one from another, as a shepherd divides *his* sheep from the goats. [c] And He will set the sheep on His right hand, but the goats on the left. [c] Then the King will say to those on His right hand, 'Come, you blessed of My Father, inherit the kingdom prepared for you from the foundation of the world: [c] for I was hungry and you gave Me food; I was thirsty and you gave Me drink; I was a stranger and you took Me in; [c] I *was* naked and you clothed Me; I was sick, and you visited Me; I was in prison and you came to Me.'**

[c] "Then the righteous will answer Him, saying, 'Lord, when did we see You hungry and feed *You,* or thirsty and give *You* drink? [c] When did we see You a stranger and take *You* in, or naked and clothe *You?* [c] Or when did we see You sick, or in prison, and come to You?' [c] And the King will answer and say to them, 'Assuredly, I say to you, inasmuch as you did *it* to one of the least of these My brethren, you did *it* to Me.'

[c] "Then He will also say to those on the left hand, 'Depart from Me, you cursed, into the everlasting fire prepared for the devil and his angels: [c] for I was hungry and you gave Me no food; I was thirsty and you gave Me no drink; [c] I was a stranger

and you did not take Me in, naked and you did not clothe Me, sick and in prison and you did not visit Me.'

[44] "Then they also will answer [d]Him, saying, 'Lord, when did we see You hungry or thirsty or a stranger or naked or sick or in prison, and did not minister to You?' [45] Then He will answer them, saying, 'Assuredly, I say to you, inasmuch as you did not do *it* to one of the least of these, you did not do *it* to Me.' [46] And these will go away into everlasting punishment, but the righteous into eternal life."

A Church Without Walls

We need to be about the work of our Father, doing what he commanded of us. We all have different gifts, different personalities, and places we fit. That is the reason God built His church. We are the body of Christ, and representing different jobs within that body is what we are to do. Finding our gifts and our purpose is paramount in our growth from milk to meat. Concentrate on your growth, study God's word, find ways to serve Him daily, and be in a constant state of prayer.

The church is what God designed to reach this world, and we are falling far short of His expectations—Heretical teachings, failure to preach God's word and adhere to its teachings, failure to reach out to our community instead of sending out teams halfway across the world, letting our closest neighbors wonder if God is there. We built stages and removed God from the streets. Where the early church sold its possessions to help others, we buy smoke machines and light shows. But Jesus did not need a building, a budget, or a brand.

We fail to stand up to the world that tells us that if we stand on God's word, we are hateful and bigoted—Refusing to stand up and say this is a sin, God's word says so. We get caught up in size and numbers, glitz and showmanship, money and stature instead of winning souls, changing hearts, and impacting others for Christ.

We need to understand that everyone we see is God's child. The addict in the street is God's child, the drunk at the bar is God's child, the young girl selling herself on the street is God's precious daughter, the homeless family living in their car is God's children and the veteran fighting the voices in their mind with a gun to their head is God's valiant warrior. We need to open our eyes to the hurt all around us, listen to the hurting voices calling from the street outside, and meet them where they are. Love them because they are a creation of our Father, and show them the same love that Christ showed us. Return mercy for mercy and show compassion as Jesus did throughout His ministry on earth.

Reflections-

Does your church resemble the early church? Do you have a church?

_____

_____

_____

What differences are there between your church and the early church?

_____

_____

_____

Is it imperative for Christians to be part of a local group of believers? Why?

_____

_____

_____

Are you involved in a small group or class at church?

_____

_____

_____

What types?

_____

_____

_____

Are you involved with any outreach?

_____

_____

_____

Could you lead someone to Christ?

_____

_____

_____

Are you ready to GO?

_____

_____

_____

Prayer for guidance

Heavenly Father, we ask that You help us to be a catalyst for change in the modern church. Give us the desire to get up and find the ways our church can reach the ones we aren't reaching today. Help us to think differently and act differently than we did yesterday. Make us a bridge between the hurting and Your church. Show us the way to impact the lives of Your children that are invisible right now. Help us to be more involved with other believers and use these relationships to reach others for You.

Amen

David Johnson

Chapter 4
Red, Brown, Yellow, Black, and White

J esus loves the little children of the world. The big children, too. They are precious in his sight, just like the children's song says. We all sang it, and we all loved it, so when did we choose to stop believing it? Living life like we aren't the same a millimeter under the skin. Hair type, skin color and other proclivities make us appear different, but only superficially. There is only one race, and that is the human race. We have ethnic and cultural differences that provide a rich cultural roux that makes life more interesting. But we allow past prejudices and injustices to mar a path forward. Instead of trying to understand differing points of view, we hunker down behind our opinions and wage a war that no one wins. This inbred hatred and unreasonable distrust keep up walls of division that hurt our families, our churches, and our nation.

This must frustrate and sadden our Lord. He came to tear down walls and build bridges between the Father and His children. At the moment of His death, the veil that separated the people from the Holy of Holies was rent from top to bottom, clearing the way for direct contact with the Father. Instead of rejoicing in our Liberty, we rebuild walls between our brothers with our own prejudices. We look at differences as obstacles rather than experiences and opportunities to learn from each other. The church needs to set an example by reaching out to neighborhoods that don't look like theirs—Evangelize in ways that reach the truly needy and invite and welcome them to their church body. Stop classifying or segregating by anything other than believer and non-believer. And only that way can we know how to love them in a manner they understand.

God loves us all, made us all, and created us all in his image. We are all equal in value and worth to our creator. God does not differentiate between races. We are held to the same standard in Romans 3:23, **"For all have sinned and come short of the glory of God."** Genesis 1:27 says God created "man" in His image: **²⁷ So God created man in His *own* image; in the image of God, He created him; male and female He created them.** It does not say that God created white men in His image or Black men in his image or brown or yellow or green. God never divides by skin color; he divides by nation and by faith. There is no mention of division by race, and this is a sin that has been driven by man's own sinful desire to propel himself at the expense of others.

When we believe, we are equal under the blood of Christ. Paul says in Galatians 3:26-29 that there is no division, only equality for those who are in Christ Jesus:

²⁶ For you are all sons of God through faith in Christ Jesus. ²⁷ For as many of you as were baptized into Christ have put on Christ. ²⁸ There is neither Jew nor Greek, there is neither slave nor free, there is neither male nor female; for you are all one in Christ Jesus. ²⁹ And if you *are* Christ's, then you are Abraham's seed, and heirs according to the promise.

There is full adoption into the family of God without exception. Even inclusion into the lineage of Jesus under Abraham's seed.

Again, in Colossians 3:8-11, Paul makes sure that the hearer knows that there is no division other than saved and unsaved. There was no bigger divide than between the circumcised and uncircumcised, Jewish and non-Jewish, but the blood of Christ usurped those divisions and closed that divide. **⁸ But now you yourselves are to put off all these: anger, wrath, malice, blasphemy, filthy language out of your mouth. ⁹ Do not lie to one another, since you have put off the old man with his deeds, ¹⁰ and have put on the new *man* who is renewed in knowledge according to the image of Him who created him, ¹¹ where there is neither Greek nor Jew, circumcised nor uncircumcised, barbarian, Scythian, slave *nor* free, but Christ *is* all and in all.** According to Paul, race does not matter, ethnicity does not matter, former faith does not matter, former sin does not matter, and social stature does not matter. The shed blood on the cross wipes away all differences, and we receive the same adoption into the family of God.

And if there was ever any doubt if there were ethnic or color differences in heaven and differences that we can see, John lays that to rest in Revelation 7:9: **⁹ After these things I looked, and behold, a great multitude which no one could number, of all nations, tribes, peoples, and tongues, standing before the throne and before the Lamb, clothed with white robes, with palm branches in their hands.**

41

If you can't get past your prejudices, Heaven may not be as perfect as you want it to be. Because, although Sunday morning is one of the most segregated hours in our country, we are walking the same narrow path to God and will spend eternity together praising and worshipping the same God. We better wake up and realize that prejudice is another form of hate, and we better repent and become colorblind. Even science agrees.

*********According to science, the % of genetics that are a reflection of appearance(race) is only .01% of our genetic makeup. Much less than skin deep, I would say.**********

Now that we have established that God does not see race or skin color as significant, are we supposed to witness to those who don't look like us? Can a black man witness to a white man successfully? And vice versa? Well, that depends on the hearts of those involved, but if we are open to being used by God and cognizant of the calling and barriers that may be present, then, of course, we can. God is in control; he breaks down barriers and walls between heaven and earth, so our tiny issue does not present a problem.

In Acts 8, Philip was sent by an angel to witness the Ethiopian Eunuch and use miracles to do it. It culminated in Philip baptizing the Ethiopian and then disappearing from the scene. Looks to me like God is in favor of a colorblind church!

[26] Now an angel of the Lord spoke to Philip, saying, "Arise and go toward the south along the road which goes down from Jerusalem to Gaza." This is [e]desert. [27] So he arose and went. And behold, a man of Ethiopia, a eunuch of great authority

under **Candace the queen of the Ethiopians, who had charge of all her treasury, and had come to Jerusalem to worship,** **²⁸ was returning. And sitting in his chariot, he was reading Isaiah the prophet. ²⁹ Then the Spirit said to Philip, "Go near and overtake this chariot…..³⁶ Now as they went down the road, they came to some water. And the eunuch said, "See,** *here* *is* **water. What hinders me from being baptized?"**

³⁷ [f]**Then Philip said, "If you believe with all your heart, you may."**

And he answered and said, "I believe that Jesus Christ is the Son of God."

³⁸ **So he commanded the chariot to stand still. And both Philip and the eunuch went down into the water, and he baptized him.**

Folks, God is calling us to be colorblind—to look beyond physical differences and instead ground our understanding in His word, rightly divided by the church. What does your circle look like?

There are challenges that are present involving the socioeconomic status between white communities and those of color. But as the middle class becomes more and more diverse and our communities begin to mirror the census, our churches better do it, too.

In too many communities, we are leaving behind bright minds that get mired in living conditions, and a cycle of poverty builds on. A non-profit focusing on breaking the cycle of poverty through education and service runs service-learning programs in several U.S. urban areas and constructs schools in developing countries. Notably, 93% of students participating in U.S. programs advance to college, and these students are twice as likely to graduate compared to their peers who do not engage in volunteer activities.

We need to be leading the call to desegregate Sunday morning, to tear down the walls that racism built. To forgive past slights, to trust based on the ultimate relationship as brothers and sisters in Christ. The world will not fix itself, and there is no one coming from the Government to repair this. They benefit from the divisions as they mark their territories and constituencies.

Again, we are missing the mark and allowing satan to divide us and keep us from being as successful in spreading the Gospel as we could be. It's time to change our thinking.

Reflections

What does your circle look like?

_____

_____

_____

If you were to begin segregating by believers and nonbelievers the way we do by color, how drastically would your circle change? We shouldn't segregate that way either, because it does not edify Christ.

_____

_____

_____

What can we do to integrate our churches?

_____

_____

_____

How can we circumvent the effects of media and government on racial relationships?

_____

_____

_____

Are there barriers in your heart that need to be torn down?

_____

_____

_____

What is the biggest hurdle in your mind that keeps us from coming together?

_____

_____

_____

Have you looked at racial issues from the view of the other side?

_____

_____

_____

Prayer:

Heavenly Father, we pray for eyes that do not see differences, do not see levels, but see Your children. Help us to see the broken through Your eyes and give us the heart to go. Lord, we pray for the opportunity to be Your hands and feet to a lost world, regardless of the hue of their skin, the change in their pocket, or the depth of their faith. Help us to love with Your compassion, to serve with Your selflessness, and to share with Your grace. Break our hearts for Your children; give us the strength of character to serve the least of these in Your name. Amen

Chapter 5

Where is the mission field?

B etter yet, where is YOUR mission field? Where in particular are YOU called? Who is YOUR neighbor? Jesus said, "Go into all the world," making disciples, baptizing, and spreading the gospel. To say everyone is to go to a foreign country and take the Gospel is to fail to recognize differences in gifts, talents and desires that are God-given to each of His children. Just as the human body has many parts, so does the body of Christ. In the same way, you don't smell with your eyes or hear with your toes, a Christ follower who can't relate to children should not get involved in nurturing children, or a male should not be the lead in counseling severely damaged females.

I know that my gifts do not lie with children; I am, by nature, not a nurturer. But I love to speak, teach, and get my hands dirty. Put me on a stage, in a classroom or running a project, and I will be a happy camper. Put me in a daycare, a hospital ward, or a nursing home, and I would feel completely out of touch. That is not where my skills lie. But it does not mean these people are not my neighbors or that I should not meet the needs that fall within my talent pool.

In his book "The Parables of Jesus," J. Dwight Pentecost spoke of Jesus' intention with the teaching of the good Samaritan. He said,

"Christ thus answered the question, 'Who is my neighbor?' by saying that any person whose need we are able to meet is our neighbor. We fulfill the righteousness of the law that demands we love our neighbor as ourselves when we respond to such a person's need according to our ability." He tied righteousness directly with the command to love your neighbor as yourself, which leads us to the realization that righteousness is not achieved if we fail to love our neighbor. If we are to prove ourselves righteous, then we must show mercy to our neighbor just as God showed us Mercy when he sent His Son to die for us. In the last line of his chapter on this parable, Dr. Pentecost says, *"Righteousness does not come through works but through the mercy of the rejected One who saw the sinner's need and responded to that need by the sacrifice of Himself."*

So, if Dr. Pentecost is correct, and I think he is, Christ is calling us to use our talents and gifts to help those whom we see need our skills. If we are aware of the need and do not do anything to help, then we are failing to love our neighbor. Pretty simple framework to successfully love your neighbor—Use what God gave you to help God's children when you see a need. We all have fundamental knowledge that there are hurting people everywhere, and we all have limited ability to meet these needs. Because of the sheer volume of need, the Christ follower must become very tuned in to the leading of the Holy Spirit and where we are called to spend our time and resources.

Because of my wife's history of mentoring and coaching girls and the fact that addiction has touched our lives in the past, we, as a couple, have a passion for those who fight addiction and abused/trafficked young women. God has called us to this space, where, time and time again, we are asked to go outside our comfort zone and into a world that does not mirror ours. But here we have found a family that loves and serves the hurting among us, where we can have our hearts ripped out when a promising life slides back into addiction or worse. This is not the glamorous mission trip to a foreign country once a year; it is a gut-wrenching, heart-warming, frustrating, and sad mission every day. We cannot give 100% of our time as some do, but we follow the leading of the Holy Spirit and show up as often as we can, supporting monetarily and with our skills and gifts where needed. (See the profiles section)

I have heard many people say, "I wish I could go on a mission trip, but money, time off, or other obligations won't let me." Our mission field starts right here, on our streets. David Wilkerson was a rural pastor who moved to New York City to help troubled youth involved in gangs and drugs. Wilkerson's efforts led to the transformation of Nicky Cruz, a notorious gang leader of the Mau Maus, through faith and compassion. Braving death threats and other violence, David loved his way into the hearts God put before him. His efforts led to many more lives being changed as both men found their Mission field on the streets of New York. (The Cross and the Switchblade)

We get caught up in thinking that the mission field is 1000 miles away when the mission field starts in your children's bedroom and right inside the walls of your own house. Paul relays this fact to fathers in Ephesians 6:4: **And you, fathers, do not provoke your children to wrath, but bring them up in the training and admonition of the Lord.** This is our first mission field and one that we will be held accountable to. The old adage still stands that the only things you can take to heaven are your wife and children.

We are also called to be witnesses by the way we raise our children. Colossians 3:21 says, **"Fathers, do not provoke your children, lest they become discouraged."** We should conduct ourselves outside our house to those that see us in positions of power or worship, **"Likewise deacons *must be* reverent, not double-tongued, not given to much wine, not greedy for money, [f] holding the[f]mystery of the faith with a pure conscience. [10] But let these also first be tested; then let them serve as deacons, being *found* blameless. [11] Likewise, *their* wives *must be* reverent, not [g]slanderers, temperate, faithful in all things. [12] Let deacons be the husbands of one wife, ruling *their* children and their own houses well." 1 Timothy 3.**

What better way to raise your children than them seeing you laying aside your time, money, and comfort to help a stranger. I still have a memory of my dad loaning money to a lady in our church to buy a car. She did not have the ability to pay him back, and he knew that. Her son, who was not a reliable guarantor, told my dad he would pay him back, but Dad knew he would never come through.

As an adult, I asked my dad if he ever got paid back, and his only response was, "No, I never reminded her about it. She thought her son was paying me." I asked, "Did he ever pay you anything?" He replied, "He never even came back to visit his mother, but at least she thought he bought her a car."

That was my dad. He would give to everybody, would witness to anybody at any time, loved the Lord, and was never ashamed to call you on your foolishness. His territories were in the worst parts of North Mississippi and Memphis, but he was never afraid. Everybody knew Mr. George and trusted him. Although he did not look like his customer, he was one of them in their eyes. All through my childhood years, I got to ride along with my dad. We went into the roughest and poorest areas, and I saw the effects of poverty, drug abuse, absentee fathers, and out-of-wedlock children – cycles of poverty that were generations deep.

But no matter what the racial, cultural, or socio-economic level of the people my dad dealt with, everyone was loved and respected by him. A customer once asked my dad why he never caught him in a lie. My dad's tongue-in-cheek response was, "I'm not smart enough to lie. I can remember the truth, but I will forget my lies." That's my dad. He found his mission field; it wasn't one everyone would have chosen, but he flourished in it and made an eternal difference.

That difference wasn't just in the lives he touched but in mine as well. My dad shaped the way I look at leadership, entrepreneurship, giving, serving, and, ultimately, what it means to be a man. My dad lived without an ego; he didn't need it because he knew who he was and where he got his value. My dad is my hero, and he is the reason I accepted Jesus at an early age and the reason that, although I rebelled as a teenager, I came back.

My dad knew his mission field; he lived a mission that some Christ followers looked down on. My dad was around the drunk, the poor, the addicted, the welfare mother, and the fatherless, and he treated them all the same and witnessed every one of them. *Where is your mission field? Who are your neighbors? Are you living an example for your children? Could you be convicted of being a Christian by those who barely know you? Is there enough evidence in your life to prosecute you for faith?*

Reflections

Do a quick search on the internet for opportunities to volunteer. List your top 3 options.

_____

_____

_____

What do you have a passion for? How can you serve the Lord there?

_____

_____

_____

When thinking of the underserved in our society, what can you do to impact their future? Show them Jesus?

_____

_____

_____

What gifts do you have that would allow you to help others?

_____

_____

_____

Prayer-

Heavenly Father, show us our field. Guide us to the neighbors that You have ordained that we reach. Help us to not falter in our outreach, capitulate to the views of others, or fail to follow Your leading. Put us in the right place to find our passion and discover the joy of serving others in Your name. Show me Your heart for these broken and dishonored lives, and then give me the intestinal fortitude to carry Your word and Your love to Your world. Create a new heart in me, O Lord, and nurture a spirit of service within my heart. Amen

Chapter 6

Bridging the Gap
Partnering for Greater Impact

―――――――――○◉○―――――――――

In a world facing increasingly complex social challenges, the need for collaboration between different sectors has never been more urgent. While both secular and religious nonprofits strive to serve their communities, their efforts often remain isolated from one another. Yet, when these two sectors join forces, their combined strengths can create a far greater impact than either could achieve alone. Let's explore how these partnerships can thrive, the barriers that sometimes get in the way, and practical ways churches can take the lead in building these relationships.

The Benefits of Collaboration

Imagine a food bank run by a secular nonprofit struggling to find enough volunteers while a nearby church has members eager to serve but lacks the logistical infrastructure to distribute food effectively. By working together, they could feed hundreds more families each month. This is just one example of how collaboration allows organizations to pool their strengths. Churches often provide volunteer networks and community trust, while secular nonprofits bring specialized expertise, broader funding sources, and evidence-based methods—creating a more effective and sustainable impact.

Partnerships also help nonprofits expand their reach. A secular organization may have resources to serve more people but may struggle to connect with certain communities. Religious groups, deeply embedded in their neighborhoods, can help bridge that gap. At the same time, collaborating with secular groups allows faith-based organizations to reach individuals who might otherwise be wary of religious institutions. This mutual exchange not only broadens each organization's influence but also fosters greater empathy and understanding between diverse groups.

But beyond practical benefits, working together offers a chance for growth. Exposure to different perspectives challenges assumptions and strengthens both partners' approaches. When secular and religious nonprofits unite around shared goals, whether fighting poverty, supporting recovery, or providing disaster relief, they can make a deeper, more lasting difference.

Barriers to Collaboration – The Jesus Thing

Despite the clear benefits, partnerships between secular and religious nonprofits aren't always easy to forge. Cultural and philosophical differences often pose the biggest hurdle. Some secular organizations fear that collaborating with religious groups might alienate their supporters or lead to unwanted proselytizing. On the other side, faith-based organizations sometimes worry that working with secular groups could force them to compromise their beliefs.

The church must understand that God does not look at the outward appearance but at the heart. Life experiences mold and make people into different embodiments of Christ. An outward appearance that is able to reach those with common backgrounds. A version that is biblically sound in its theology but packaged in a way that puts at ease those who are suspicious of the version that looks perfect and proper.

The addict coming out of rehab needs someone with an understanding of his demons and someone who does not judge his past. A person who values his experiences because they made him who he is now. The scared girl coming off the streets will have little in common with the girls at the high school. Jaded and used by others, the chances are that her abusers looked like the people sitting in the pews on Sunday. These children of God need understanding and outreach that does not intimidate and push but loves them into the arms of God.

In the same way, secular organizations need to understand the value that faith brings to recovery, pain, and suffering. The love of Jesus is supernatural and can change hearts when the person hears the truth of Jesus. Old hurts, biases and betrayals breed distrust in some who refuse to accept the sincerity of the Church. They must understand that true Christ followers know that the only difference between themselves and unbelievers is forgiveness. A partnership that starts with basic trust and understanding will withstand old opinions and forge new relationships that will make both camps better and more effective.

Communication and trust are additional stumbling blocks. Misunderstandings about each other's motives or operational practices can lead to friction. Language differences—both literal and cultural—can make it harder to find common ground. And then there's the issue of pride: both secular and religious nonprofits often take great pride in their work, which can sometimes translate into a reluctance to share credit or cede control.

Legal restrictions

Legal and regulatory challenges can also complicate matters. Many government grants prohibit using funds for religious activities, which can limit how religious nonprofits participate in joint initiatives. Differences in governance structures and compliance requirements further add to the complexity.

Building Successful Partnerships

Overcoming these barriers starts with finding common ground. At the core, both secular and religious nonprofits share a commitment to serving others. By focusing on this shared mission, they can build partnerships that respect each other's differences while amplifying their collective impact.

Clear, open communication is essential. Both parties should discuss expectations, boundaries, and concerns from the outset to avoid misunderstandings down the line. Defining each partner's roles and responsibilities ensures that efforts are complementary rather than overlapping. Formal agreements can help clarify these details, including protocols for decision-making and conflict resolution.

Mutual respect is key. Both partners must approach the relationship with humility, recognizing that they have much to learn from one another. Providing opportunities for cross-cultural training can help bridge philosophical differences and foster empathy. By celebrating each other's strengths and avoiding judgment, secular and religious nonprofits can create partnerships built on trust and collaboration.

Christians must be aware that often hurts and life's mishaps create a dissonance between a person and God. Looking around to place blame, people often latch on to the idea that God should have stopped a situation, and the animosity grows in their hearts, creating barriers that are not easily breached.

At times, secular institutions are the catalyst to exponential reach, but they need to understand that the mission of the church is to save the body, with the ultimate goal of saving the soul. The secular organizations must understand that the overarching view of the church is that saving the body is a temporary reprieve, and without salvation, the soul of the person is still lost, and eternity is far more precious than this life. (see chapter 10, We don't set the pace)

How Churches Can Initiate Outreach

Churches are uniquely positioned to take the first step in building these partnerships. Start by identifying local secular nonprofits with missions that align with your church's values. Look for organizations addressing issues like homelessness, addiction recovery, or youth development—areas where churches often have both passion and resources to offer.

When reaching out, approach with humility and openness. Emphasize that your goal is to serve the community together, not necessarily to promote a religious agenda. Respect the secular organization's values and operational practices, even if they differ from your own.

Offer tangible support, whether by providing volunteers, hosting events, or sharing physical space. Avoid attaching strings to your assistance—true partnership means giving without expecting anything in return. Start small with joint projects to build trust and demonstrate reliability. As the relationship grows, explore opportunities for long-term collaboration.

Finally, share the success stories that result from these partnerships. Highlighting the positive impact of working together can inspire other churches and nonprofits to follow suit. The more these stories are told, the more normalized—and celebrated—such collaborations will become.

By bridging the gap between secular and religious nonprofits, we can create a world where compassion and expertise go hand in hand. Though challenges may arise, they are far outweighed by the benefits of working together to serve those in need. Now is the time to set aside differences and focus on what unites us – a shared commitment to making the world a better, more compassionate place. Whether through a food bank, a homeless shelter, or a youth mentoring program, the partnerships we build today will shape a more hopeful future for all.

Reflections:

What organizations have you overlooked that may present a partnership that you previously discounted?

_____

_____

_____

What do you see as the single most important thing that could come from a partnership outside of the faith community?

_____

_____

_____

How do you envision a new relationship helping the ultimate goal of leading others to Christ?

_____

_____

_____

Do you see the value in trusting God's timing in reaching the lost as you work within parameters that may not allow overt witnessing? Explain.

_____

_____

_____

Prayer:

Heavenly Father, open my eyes to see all Your children. To love with your heart and see with Your eyes. Forgive my judgmental spirit and help me to accept those who are different than me, who have different backgrounds than me, and understand that they are Your children and called to help just like me. Wipe away the outward and open my heart to the inward and see the heart, the intent, and the works. Help me to bridge the divide with those who can serve Your purpose even if we don't share a common faith. Help me to live a Christ-like life that shines like a light on the hill and flavors the world with Your richness. Amen

David Johnson

Chapter 7

Playing Favorites

I heard a story about a rather large church in an influential neighborhood that had just hired a new pastor. The church was all abuzz about their new leader, and excitement filled the air. The young pastor was excited as well. He had gotten into town several days ahead of the weekend and spent much time walking the city and learning his way around. It was noticeable that it was a prosperous place; the parks were manicured, the streets swept, and the storefronts well-kept.

He began to notice the lack of diversity. He didn't see the poor or less successful around town, so he expanded his exploration until he reached the outskirts of town. There, he found dirtier streets, unkempt parks and sidewalks; the difference was staggering. He parked his car and got out and walked the street, talking to the neighbors, learning that his church and town were not a welcoming place for them. They were not made to feel welcome and stayed on their own side of town.

The new pastor left disheartened, wondering what he had gotten himself into with a church that did not welcome everyone and had such a bad reputation. He pondered what to do until, finally, he had an idea.

Sunday morning came, and the pastor readied himself to be introduced to the church with plans to address the disparity in the town. He had invited many of the people from the other side of town and hoped to see some of them.

As the church members began showing up for the morning service, anticipation grew as they looked forward to meeting their new pastor. But as the congregants neared the front of the sanctuary, they noticed a very disheveled man sitting on the bench near the door. He had a scraggly beard; his hair was covered with a soiled skull cap; his clothes were tattered and torn, and his shoes were hardly more than pieces of cardboard. Before him was a collection of items for sale with a sign that said, *"Homeless, please buy my crafts."*

As the congregation filed by him, they looked on in distaste at the man, wondering why he would come to sit in front of the church where families were going to worship. The ladies tsked and shook their heads, and the men frowned and moved their families to the other side of the walk.

As the churchgoers settled into their pews, putting away their bibles and shushing their kids, they noticed the disheveled man from the bench shuffling down the center aisle, leaning heavily on an old, weathered cane, headed toward the front of the church. Some people pointed, and some snickered as he finally reached the front pew and lowered himself down onto the bench. One of the deacons, worried that the man may cause trouble, made his way to the front and sat at the other end of the pew, watching the man.

The music swelled, and the choir sang; the offering was taken, and a prayer was given. As the head of the pastor search committee rose and prepared to introduce the new pastor, the people craned their necks to glimpse the new pastor. A hush fell over the congregation as no one stood up. Where was the pastor? Necks craned, heads turned, and whispering started.

Suddenly, the disheveled man rose from the first row and slowly, painfully climbed the stairs to the pulpit. He turned to face the congregation, gripped the sides of the pulpit, and introduced himself.

"Good morning, I'm pastor Franks, and it is always a pleasure to be in the house of the Lord."

He reached up to his beard and slowly removed the epoxied hair from his face. "I'm sorry to come in disguise, but I wanted to get a feel for the kind of church we had here. See, I spent most of my day yesterday dressed like this in our town and was surprised that no matter where I went, I was ignored or asked to leave. No one asked me if I needed help, was hungry, or sick, and no one bought my crafts. I thought, surely this is not our congregation moving to the other side of the street to be away from me. Surely, they would show me love, offer me help, and show concern."

He continued, "But as I sat in front of this beautiful sanctuary this morning, I was treated the same, with open disdain but no pity. I felt ill as I remembered Jesus' claim that the second greatest commandment is to love your neighbor as yourself. We have a lot of work to do to be what this community deserves us to be."

With that, the pastor picked up his cane and walked down the stairs, down the aisle, and out of the church. The congregation looked at each other, wondering what had just happened. Was that really the pastor's first sermon? Was it over? Was it time to go home?

Slowly, an elderly lady rose from the third row and climbed the stairs to the pulpit. She reached up and lowered the mic so it would pick up her frail voice. She cleared her throat, and in a broken emotional voice, she said, "I saw him yesterday, sitting by the tracks all alone. I thought to myself, what must he have done to end up dirty and homeless like that? In my heart, I was angry that he was there. My heart was so hard that God could not even speak to me. I have been so wrong." As she finished speaking, she noticeably sobbed and wiped her eyes.

She slowly made her way back down the steps and, at the bottom, sank to her knees and began to pray for forgiveness. Slowly, others joined her until there was a wholesale break as hearts were broken and convicted. The altar filled, tears were shed, and hearts were changed.

Across town, the preacher slipped into the back of a church and sat in the back row. He was welcomed with smiles and handshakes. One of the young men brought him a church bulletin and asked to sit with him. The pastor's eyes filled with tears as he bowed his head and worshipped in a building full of people who did not look like him.

The way I heard it, the town changed that day with programs designed to bring churches together, repair relationships, and bridge the gap between neighbors. One pastor's courage to call his brand-new flock out and go where he knew he needed to go made a difference.

I'm not sure how much of that story is true, but I do know that there are churches just like that all over our nation and congregations that want to be entertained and encouraged but never challenged. In most churches like that one, the pastor would have probably been asked to resign before the next Sunday.

In other churches, you have your core group of members who do all the work. Teach the classes, serve on the committees, keep the nursery, and do the outreach. Most churches are understaffed by volunteers, creating burnout in the core group that will serve. Christ's followers need to step up, lean in, and serve the Lord with the talents that God gave them. Teaching, serving, and praying for the least of those around us, regardless of their station in life, ethnic differences, past, or socio-economic status.

So often, we as the church have forgotten where we came from, who we were before God saved us. We are so intent on checking boxes that we fail to check our hearts. Is the low-income apartment building down the street welcome to send their kids to your Sunday school? Does the single mom feel that she can worship without being judged? The addict in treatment, the convict on parole, can be forgiven just as we were.

Remember that we worship the same Jesus who washed the feet of the person that he knew had already betrayed Him, the same Holy person who gave up their life as a ransom for many.

James 2 tells us what we should be.

My brethren, do not hold the faith of our Lord Jesus Christ, T*he Lord* of glory, with partiality. [2] For if there should come into your assembly a man with gold rings, in [a]fine apparel, and there should also come in a poor man in [b]filthy clothes, [3] and you [c]pay attention to the one wearing the fine clothes and say to him, "You sit here in a good place," and say to the poor man, "You stand there," or, "Sit here at my footstool," [4] have you not [d]shown partiality among yourselves, and become judges with evil thoughts?

[5] Listen, my beloved brethren: Has God not chosen the poor of this world *to be* rich in faith and heirs of the kingdom which He promised to those who love Him? [6] But you have dishonored the poor man. Do not the rich oppress you and drag you into the courts? [7] Do they not blaspheme that noble name by which you are called?

[8] If you really fulfill *the* royal law according to the Scripture, "You shall love your neighbor as yourself," you do well; [9] but if you [e]show partiality, you commit sin, and are convicted by the law as transgressors. [10] For whoever shall keep the whole law, and yet stumble in one *point,* he is guilty of all. [11] For He who said, "Do not commit adultery," also said, "Do not murder." Now if you do not commit adultery, but you do

murder, you have become a transgressor of the law. [12] So speak and so do as those who will be judged by the law of liberty. [13] For judgment is without mercy to the one who has shown no mercy. Mercy triumphs over judgment.

[14] What *does it* profit, my brethren, if someone says he has faith but does not have works? Can faith save him? [15] If a brother or sister is naked and destitute of daily food, [16] and one of you says to them, "Depart in peace, be warmed and filled," but you do not give them the things which are needed for the body, what *does it* profit? [17] Thus also faith by itself, if it does not have works, is dead.

[18] But someone will say, "You have faith, and I have works." Show me your faith without [f]your works, and I will show you my faith by [g]my works. [19] You believe that there is one God. You do well. Even the demons believe—and tremble! [20] But do you want to know, O foolish man, that faith without works is [h]dead? [21] Was not Abraham our father justified by works when he offered Isaac his son on the altar? [22] Do you see that faith was working together with his works, and by works faith was made [i]perfect? [23] And the Scripture was fulfilled which says, "Abraham believed God, and it was [j]accounted to him for righteousness." And he was called the friend of God. [24] You see then that a man is justified by works, and not by faith only.

²⁵ Likewise, was not Rahab the harlot also justified by works when she received the messengers and sent *them* out another way?

²⁶ For as the body without the spirit is dead, so faith without works is dead also.

James addresses the issue of partiality and discrimination within the Christian community, emphasizing the importance of treating others with equality and fairness, both in the sight of man and God.

The chapter begins by condemning the practice of showing favoritism to the wealthy while treating the poor with disdain. James argues that such behavior contradicts the essence of the Christian faith, which teaches love, compassion, and justice for all.

In verses 1-7, James criticizes the behavior of those who give preferential treatment to the rich while ignoring or mistreating the poor. He points out that this attitude is not only unjust but also sinful, as it goes against the commandment to love one's neighbor as oneself.

James illustrates his point with an example of a scenario where a wealthy man is given special treatment and a prominent seat in the assembly, while a poor man is relegated to a lowly position or even treated with contempt. He challenges the readers to reflect on their own biases and prejudices and reminds them that God has chosen the poor to be rich in faith and the heirs of the kingdom.

Furthermore, James emphasizes the principle of equality before God. Regardless of social status or material wealth, all individuals are equally accountable to God and will be judged based on their actions and attitudes. He warns against showing partiality, reminding the readers that mercy triumphs over judgment.

In verses 14-26, James extends his discussion to the relationship between faith and works, emphasizing that genuine faith is demonstrated through actions. He argues that faith without deeds is dead, likening it to a body without spirit. In this context, treating others with equality and fairness is not just a matter of moral obligation but also a tangible expression of one's faith in action.

Overall, James chapter 2 underscores the importance of treating others with equality and fairness, regardless of their social status or background. It highlights the principle of impartiality as a core value of the Christian faith and emphasizes the inseparable link between faith and works in demonstrating genuine devotion to God.

If faith without works is dead, the church is on life support

There cannot be any confusion that there is no salvation by works; works do not save; they are the evidence of faith in a believer's life. The only way to the Father is through the Son. His shed blood on the cross is the propitiation for our sins. Without that payment, we are still dead in our sins, and we have no relationship with the Father.

But because we have accepted Christ as our Savior, we are now called to love our neighbors, all of them. With no preference for the rich, famous, or influential, we are to see everyone through the eyes of Jesus. If we see through the eyes of Jesus, we see value in the Children, in people with a "history," in the hated, and in the infirm. Because Jesus said, "Let the children come to me," he spent time with the woman at the well, Matthew (a tax collector) and the cripple, possessed and diseased. Jesus was called the great physician because He tended to the broken, not the best; the downtrodden, not the successful; the lost, not the religious; the sick, not the firm.

Commit yourself to loving by God's standard.

Reflections

Have you ever noticed preferential treatment in your church? Did you point it out?

_____

_____

_____

How can we, as a church, protect against showing partiality to our members?

_____

_____

_____

When you see someone who is homeless, what is your first reaction and thought?

_____

_____

_____

What do you think God would have you do with the panhandler?

_____

_____

_____

Prayer:

Heavenly Father, help us to have a heart for those in our circles who are suffering, whether it is their problem, why they are there, or circumstances beyond their control. Help us to have compassion. Help us to look at them as Your children with intrinsic value, worthy of our time and effort. Slow us down and remind us to love with our hearts, lend a hand where it is needed, and speak respectfully to everyone. Build in us a sense of urgency for the lost with no stipulations so that we may take Your Gospel to those who need it most. Amen.

Chapter 8
Jesus Talks to the Churches

———————⌒⊙⌒———————

In the Book of Revelation, God, through Jesus Christ, delivers messages to seven churches in Asia Minor. Each church receives a unique message tailored to its spiritual condition, and these messages are found in Revelation chapters 2 and 3:

1. **Ephesus**: Commended for hard work and perseverance, but criticized for losing their first love. They are urged to repent and return to their initial devotion (Revelation 2:1-7).

2. **Smyrna**: Commended for their suffering and poverty but spiritual richness. They are encouraged to remain faithful even unto death, with the promise of the crown of life (Revelation 2:8-11).

3. **Pergamum**: Commended for holding fast to Christ's name despite living where Satan's throne is. However, they are criticized for tolerating false teachings and immoral practices. They are called to repent (Revelation 2:12-17).

4. **Thyatira**: Commended for their love, faith, service, and perseverance. However, they are criticized for tolerating the false prophetess Jezebel, who leads them into immorality. They are urged to repent and hold fast until Christ's return (Revelation 2:18-29).

5. **Sardis**: Criticized for being spiritually dead despite having a reputation for being alive. They are called to wake up, strengthen what remains, and repent (Revelation 3:1-6).

6. **Philadelphia**: Commended for their deeds and for keeping Christ's word and not denying His name. They are encouraged with promises of protection and honor, with no criticisms given (Revelation 3:7-13).

7. **Laodicea**: Criticized for being lukewarm, neither hot nor cold. They are urged to be zealous and repent, with Christ offering to come in and dine with those who open the door to Him (Revelation 3:14-22).

All but two churches received a level of rebuke for faltering in their role as salt and light in the world. Let's look at these 5 and see what God tells the modern church through His words to the churches in Revelation.

Ephesus – losing our first love

The church of Ephesus, addressed in Revelation 2:1-7, was one of the seven churches in Asia Minor to which Jesus sent messages through the Apostle John. The Ephesian church was commended for its hard work, perseverance, and rejection of false teachings. However, despite these commendable attributes, Jesus rebuked them for having forsaken their "first love."

The "first love" refers to the initial fervor and passion the Ephesian believers had for Christ and for one another when they first came to faith. This love is characterized by an intense, heartfelt devotion and an eagerness to follow Jesus and serve others. Over time, however, this initial zeal had waned, and their relationship with Christ had become more about duty and orthodoxy than about a loving, personal relationship. They continued to do the right things, but lacked the love and passion that originally motivated their actions.

Over time, routine can lead to a mechanical approach to faith, where actions are performed out of habit rather than love. The Ephesian church was diligent in maintaining correct doctrine and refuting false teachings, which is essential. However, an excessive focus on doctrine can sometimes overshadow the relational aspect of faith, turning love for neighbor into mere duty and causing people to be seen as obligations rather than individuals.

The early church faced significant external pressures and persecutions, which could cause believers to shift focus from their internal spiritual health to external survival and defense. In today's world, we are faced with a world that is devoid of Christ in much of our society, and we are made to feel that if we stand on God's word, we are bigoted or prejudiced. In our busy world, the failure to engage in personal spiritual practices like prayer, worship, and meditating on God's Word can lead to a gradual cooling of spiritual fervor.

Jesus provides a clear pathway for the Ephesian church (and, by extension, any believer or church experiencing a similar loss of passion) to return to their first love. Jesus instructs the Ephesians to "consider how far you have fallen" (Revelation 2:5a, NIV). This involves reflecting on the early days of their faith, remembering the fervor, joy, and love they once had for Christ and for one another. Recognizing and acknowledging the change in their spiritual state is the first step toward restoration.

He calls for repentance, which involves a sincere turning away from the attitudes and behaviors that led to the loss of love. This means rejecting complacency, routine, and any form of legalism that has replaced genuine affection for Christ. To confess this state to God, ask for forgiveness, and seek His help to reignite their love and passion.

Jesus advises them to "do the things you did at first" (Revelation 2:5b, NIV). This means returning to spiritual disciplines and practices that foster intimacy with God. Spend quality time in prayer— not just presenting requests but cultivating a loving dialogue with Him. Engage in heartfelt worship, both personally and with others, to rekindle a sense of awe and love for God. Immerse yourself in His Word to reconnect with His promises, commands, and the story of redemption. Finally, serve others with the love of Christ, not out of obligation but out of a genuine desire to reflect His love to the world.

Re-engage with the world in a meaningful way, participating in mutual encouragement, accountability, and support. Demonstrate love through acts of kindness, generosity, and compassion, both within the church and in the broader community. Truly love your neighbor as Christ commanded.

God's words to the church at Ephesus are a timeless warning and encouragement for all believers. Losing one's first love for Christ can happen subtly over time due to routine, external pressures, and a focus on form over relationship. However, Jesus' call to remember, repent, and return offers a clear pathway to restoration. By reigniting their love through intentional spiritual practices and a renewed focus on their relationship with Christ, believers can once again experience the fervor and passion of their initial encounter with Jesus, enhancing their impact on the lives in their communities profoundly.

Pergamum accepting false teaching.

The church of Pergamum presents valuable insights for contemporary believers. This church, located in a city known for its cultural and religious diversity, faced unique challenges that led to both commendation and rebuke from Christ. Pergamum (modern-day Bergama in Turkey) was a prominent city in ancient Asia Minor, renowned for its library and temples and as a center of emperor worship. The city was filled with altars of various gods, including Zeus and Asclepius, making it a challenging environment for Christians to maintain their faith. As God talked to the seven churches, he singled out Pergamum and their acceptance of false teachings and watered-down faith.

Revelation 2:12-13: To the angel of the church in Pergamum write: These are the words of him who has the sharp, double-edged sword. I know where you live—where Satan has his throne. Yet you remain true to my name. You did not renounce your faith in me, not even in the days of Antipas, my faithful witness, who was put to death in your city—where Satan lives. Nevertheless, I have a few things against you: There are some among you who hold to the teaching of Balaam, who taught Balak to entice the Israelites to sin so that they ate food sacrificed to idols and committed sexual immorality. Likewise, you also have those who hold to the teaching of the Nicolaitans. Repent, therefore! Otherwise, I will soon come to you and will fight against them with the sword of my mouth.

God commends the believers in Pergamum for their steadfastness and faithfulness despite living in a city rife with idolatry and persecution. They remained true to Christ's name even when faced with the martyrdom of Antipas, a prominent member of their church. But despite their faithfulness, the church is rebuked for allowing false teachings to infiltrate their community. The teachings of Balaam and the Nicolaitans led some believers to engage in idolatry and sexual immorality, compromising their faith.

Just like the early church, today, many of us find ourselves in congregations that refuse to condemn sin in our world for fear of being labeled bigoted or hateful. But refusing to stand on the teaching of Jesus and the New Testament is tearing at the very fabric of our faith. Prosperity gospel and churches that accept sin that is called out as abominations to God are leading people astray and failing to show the church as set apart or different in our world.

God calls the church to repent and turn away from these false teachings and immoral practices. The warning is clear: failure to repent will result in Christ Himself coming to judge them with the "sword of His mouth," symbolizing the power and authority of His word. But for those who overcome and remain faithful, God promises hidden manna, symbolizing spiritual sustenance, and the white stone with a new name, symbolizing acceptance, acquittal, and a personal relationship with God.

The believers in Pergamum are commended for their steadfast faith in a hostile environment. Modern Christians can learn the importance of remaining true to their faith even when surrounded by cultural pressures and opposition. Faithfulness to Christ should not waver, even in the face of persecution or societal challenges. The rebuke to Pergamum underscores the danger of allowing false teachings and practices to infiltrate the church. The same warning applies today. Believers must stay vigilant, discerning truth from deception. Holding firmly to biblical teachings is essential, as is rejecting any doctrine that compromises faith and morals.

God's call to repentance highlights the importance of acknowledging and turning away from sin. For contemporary believers, regular self-examination and repentance are crucial in maintaining the right relationship with God and staying true to His commandments. The warning of judgment and the promise of reward serve as a reminder that God is both just and gracious. While He will judge those who persist in sin, He also promises abundant blessings to those who remain faithful. This dual assurance should motivate believers to live righteously and persevere in their faith. The promise of a white stone with a new name signifies a unique, personal relationship with

God. This encourages believers to seek a deep, intimate connection with Him, knowing that their identity and worth are found in Christ.

The message to the church of Pergamum offers profound lessons for today's church. It highlights the importance of steadfast faithfulness in the face of opposition, vigilance against false teachings, the necessity of repentance, and the assurance of both divine judgment and reward. By applying these lessons, contemporary believers can navigate the challenges of a secular world, maintain the purity of their faith, and foster a deep, personal relationship with God. Through the example of Pergamum, the church is encouraged to stand firm, discern truth, and seek continuous growth in their spiritual journey.

Thyatira Watered Down Faith

The church of Thyatira provides important insights for contemporary believers. Thyatira was a city in Asia Minor (modern-day Turkey), renowned for its industries, particularly textiles and dyeing. The city was a center of trade and commerce, with numerous trade guilds that often involved pagan practices and idol worship, making it a challenging environment for Christians to maintain their faith amidst prevailing cultural and social influences. The Christian community in Thyatira faced significant pressure to conform to these practices. Sound familiar?

Revelation 2:18-29: To the angel of the church in Thyatira, write: These are the words of the Son of God, whose eyes are like blazing fire and whose feet are like burnished bronze. I know your deeds, your love and faith, your service and perseverance, and that you are now doing more than you did at first. Nevertheless, I have this against you: You tolerate that woman Jezebel, who calls herself a prophet. By her teaching she misleads my servants into sexual immorality and the eating of food sacrificed to idols. I have given her time to repent of her immorality, but she is unwilling. So I will cast her on a bed of suffering, and I will make those who commit adultery with her suffer intensely, unless they repent of her ways. I will strike her children dead. Then all the churches will know that I am he who searches hearts and minds, and I will repay each of you according to your deeds. Now I say to the rest of you in Thyatira, to you who do not hold to her teaching and have not learned Satan's so-called deep secrets, 'I will not impose any other burden on you, except to hold on to what you have until I come. To the one who is victorious and does my will to the end, I will give authority over the nations—'He will rule them with an iron scepter and will dash them to pieces like pottery'—just as I have received authority from my Father. I will also give that one the morning star. Whoever has ears, let them hear what the Spirit says to the churches.

God commends the believers in Thyatira for their love, faith, service, perseverance, and growth in good works. Despite the challenges they faced, they continued to demonstrate these virtues, showing progress in their spiritual journey. But despite their commendable deeds, the church is rebuked for tolerating the false teachings of a woman symbolically named Jezebel. This false prophetess led believers into immorality and idolatry. God's rebuke emphasizes the seriousness of tolerating sin and false doctrine within the church. God acknowledges those who have not succumbed to Jezebel's teachings and encourages them to hold fast to their faith and continue resisting false doctrines. God promises those who remain faithful will receive authority and the morning star, symbolizing victory, honor, and eternal fellowship with Christ.

The commendation of the Thyatira church for their love, faith, service, and perseverance highlights the importance of these virtues in the Christian life. Believers today are encouraged to continually grow in their faith, demonstrating their commitment through acts of love and service. But we also must guard against false doctrine and diluted teaching.

Because quickly following His commendation was God's rebuke of the Thyatira church for tolerating Jezebel's teachings. This should serve as a stern warning against allowing sin and false doctrine to persist within the church. Contemporary believers must be vigilant in identifying and addressing false teachings and immoral practices that can lead the community astray. Because although they were doing so many things right, they still missed the mark.

So many of today's churches sacrifice sound teaching to attract big crowds. Churches have become businesses that assume getting people in the door is just as important as teaching them the Gospel. Relying on music to stimulate the hearts instead of trusting God's word and the Holy Spirit to work in the hearts of the listeners. You can turn on your TV and watch a whole church service without ever hearing the name of Jesus from the pulpit. Or hear that if you only ask, you will receive everything you want now. God forgive us for ever misleading His children.

Just as God calls for repentance from those misled by Jezebel, it underscores the necessity of turning away from sin and returning to righteousness. Believers today must practice regular self-examination and repentance to maintain a pure and faithful relationship with God.

The encouragement to hold fast to what they have until Christ comes highlights the importance of perseverance. Believers are called to remain steadfast in their faith, resisting pressures to conform to ungodly practices and teachings. We must test the words of our leaders to ensure that we are hearing the truth.

The message to the church of Thyatira offers profound lessons for contemporary believers. It emphasizes the importance of good works, spiritual growth, vigilance against false teachings, the necessity of repentance, perseverance in faith, and the assurance of divine reward. By applying these lessons, the modern church can navigate the challenges of a secular and often compromising world, maintain the purity of its faith, and foster a deep, enduring relationship with God. Through the example of Thyatira, believers are encouraged to uphold righteousness, resist falsehood, and remain faithful to their calling in Christ.

Sardis Going soft

The church at Sardis was one of the seven churches addressed by Jesus through John in the Book of Revelation. Sardis was a wealthy city known for its softness and luxury, but also for its complacency. The message to the church reflects these characteristics and serves as both a warning and a call to renewal.

Revelation 3:1-5: I know your works; you have a reputation of being alive, but you are dead. Wake up, and strengthen what remains and is about to die, for I have not found your works complete in the sight of my God. Remember, then, what you received and heard. Keep it, and repent. If you will not wake up, I will come like a thief, and you will not know at what hour I will come against you. Yet you have still a few names in Sardis, people who have not soiled their garments, and they will walk with me in white, for they are worthy. The one who conquers will be clothed thus in white garments, and I will never blot his name out of the book of life. I will confess his name before my Father and before his angels.

There is a significant difference between outward appearance and inner reality. The church in Sardis had a good reputation but was spiritually dead. The importance of self-examination and authenticity in faith and practice cannot be overlooked in our walk. Spiritual vigilance is crucial. Complacency and spiritual slumber can lead to decay. This calls for continuous growth and renewal in one's spiritual life. Reflecting on and adhering to foundational teachings is essential.

Repentance and returning to core principles can restore spiritual vitality. The consequences of spiritual neglect are serious and often sudden. This underscores the need for preparedness and a consistent walk with God. Faithfulness, even in a context of widespread complacency, is recognized and rewarded by God. This encourages perseverance in righteousness. Overcoming spiritual challenges leads to eternal rewards and acknowledgment by Christ. This offers hope and motivation to remain steadfast.

Below are 6 steps to protect from the spiritual softness and decay that God warned the church at Sardis about:

1. Self-Examination: Regularly assess personal and communal spiritual health beyond outward appearances.

2. Spiritual Vigilance: Stay alert and proactive in nurturing one's faith to prevent stagnation and decline.

3. Adherence to Core Teachings: Continually revisit and apply foundational Christian teachings and principles.

4. Preparedness: Live in readiness for Christ's return by maintaining a vibrant and active faith.

5. Faithfulness in Adversity: Uphold righteousness and integrity, even when surrounded by complacency or corruption.

6. Hope in Eternal Reward: Draw strength from the promises of eternal life and divine recognition for overcoming challenges.

The message to the church at Sardis is a timeless reminder of the dangers of spiritual complacency and the importance of authenticity, vigilance, repentance, and faithfulness. By internalizing these lessons, individuals and communities can strive for a more vibrant and resilient spiritual life.

Laodicea Lukewarm spirituality

Laodicea was a wealthy city known for its banking, textile, and medical industries. The church in Laodicea is the only one among the seven churches in Revelation to receive no commendation, only rebuke, highlighting the seriousness of its spiritual condition and offering important lessons on spiritual fervor, self-awareness, and dependence on Christ.

Revelation 3:15-21: I know your works: you are neither cold nor hot. Would that you were either cold or hot! So, because you are lukewarm, and neither hot nor cold, I will spit you out of my mouth. For you say, I am rich, I have prospered, and I need nothing, not realizing that you are wretched, pitiable, poor, blind, and naked. I counsel you to buy from me gold refined by fire, so that you may be rich, and white garments so that you may clothe yourself and the shame of your nakedness may not be seen, and salve to anoint your eyes, so that you may see. Those whom I love, I reprove and discipline, so be zealous and repent. Behold, I stand at the door and knock. If anyone hears my voice and opens the door, I will come in to him and eat with him, and he with me. The one who conquers, I will grant him to sit with me on my throne, as I also conquered and sat down with my Father on his throne.

Indifference and complacency in faith are unacceptable to God. A passionate and committed faith is essential. The church should strive to be fervent in its devotion and actions. Material wealth and self-sufficiency can lead to spiritual blindness. The church must recognize its true spiritual condition and its need for God, regardless of worldly prosperity. True spiritual wealth comes from God. Pursue spiritual richness, righteousness, and clarity of vision by seeking Christ's provision.

God's rebuke is an act of love intended to bring about repentance and renewal. The church should respond to correction with zeal and genuine repentance. Christ desires intimate fellowship with His followers. The church should be open and responsive to His call, fostering a deep and personal relationship with Him. Overcoming spiritual lukewarmness and complacency leads to a share in Christ's victory and authority. This promise motivates believers to strive for spiritual excellence.

Here are 6 steps for combating becoming lukewarm

1. **Reject Spiritual Complacency:** The church must actively cultivate a passionate and committed faith, avoiding indifference and complacency.

2. **Acknowledge Spiritual Needs:** Recognize that material wealth and self-sufficiency can mask spiritual poverty. Acknowledge the need for God's grace and provision.

3. **Seek Spiritual Richness:** Prioritize spiritual growth and seek the true riches that come from a relationship with Christ, including righteousness and spiritual insight.

4. **Embrace Correction:** View God's reproof as an act of love and respond with sincere repentance and renewed zeal for His purposes.

5. **Cultivate Intimacy with Christ:** Open the door to Christ's presence in every aspect of life, fostering a close and personal relationship with Him.

6. **Strive for Overcoming:** Aim to overcome challenges and spiritual complacency, inspired by the promise of sharing in Christ's victory and authority.

The message to the church in Laodicea is a powerful call to self-awareness, repentance, and wholehearted devotion. By learning from Laodicea's mistakes and embracing the counsel given, today's church can avoid spiritual complacency and experience a vibrant and fulfilling relationship with Christ.

Reflections

How do you see your current walk with God? Do you still maintain your first love? Do you still have your original fervor and passion for Him? Why or why not?

_____

_____

_____

What system do you use to weigh the teachings you hear? What teachers do you stay away from?

_____

_____

_____

What do you feel are the most destructive false teachings in our society?

_____

_____

_____

How do you protect yourself from watering down your faith? Making exceptions and excuses in your own life?

_____

_____

_____

How do you protect yourself from becoming lukewarm in your faith? Do you currently feel that you are walking close to Him, serving your neighbor, and following His will for your life? Why?

_____

_____

_____

Prayer

Dear Heavenly Father, help my divided heart. Help me to stay focused on Your will and not mine. Let me not become lukewarm, in danger of Your anger, but help me to retain the fervor of my first love. Renew in me a right heart, one that follows You and yearns for a closer walk each day. Forgive my willingness to accept half-truths and watered-down convictions. Don't let my eye wander to others in judgment, but focus on my own brokenness and failures. Amen

Chapter 9

Finishing at the Starting Line

━━━━━━━━━━━━━━⌒◉⌒━━━━━━━━━━━━━━

The churches that Jesus spoke to in Revelation had been active for some time and had the teaching of the apostles and disciples who knew Jesus. We are not going to begin with that strength of faith, but with practice, study and communion with Jesus, we can certainly mature into vessels that can serve our Lord's needs. Your daily walk is like an athlete's practice or money in the bank, and it adds strength or compounds daily.

When runners come to the starting line for a race, it is the culmination of months and years of preparation. The runner has spent a whole lifetime training for that moment in the starting blocks. Likewise, a musician playing a song is not an impromptu thing. He has spent years learning to play an instrument, read music, and practice that song. In the same way, Christians need to prepare themselves to serve others, draw insights from the life and teachings of Jesus, explore the foundational commandment to love our neighbor as ourselves and examine how this principle permeates our faith. By reflecting on Jesus' life, we underscore the significance of service as a central tenet of our relationship with Christ and embrace a life of sacrificial love and service.

The essence of Christianity is rooted in love—love for God and love for others. Central to this love is the commandment Jesus gave: to love our neighbor as ourselves. In this book, we explored why Christians need to prepare themselves to serve others, inspired by the life and teachings of Jesus Christ, as the life of Jesus serves as the ultimate model for Christian service.

Throughout his earthly ministry, Jesus demonstrated compassion, humility, and selflessness in his interactions with others. He healed the sick, comforted the afflicted, and showed mercy to the marginalized. Jesus' entire life was a testament to the principle of serving others.

Philippians 2:5-8 shows the expectation of the level of love we should have for one another: **"In your relationships with one another, have the same mindset as Christ Jesus: Who, being in very nature God, did not consider equality with God something to be used to his own advantage; rather, he made himself nothing by taking the very nature of a servant, being made in human likeness. And being found in appearance as a man, he humbled himself by becoming obedient to death— even death on a cross!"**

So, how did Jesus love? How did His love manifest itself in His ministry? Here are 4 ways:

1. **Compassion for the Marginalized:** Jesus consistently demonstrated compassion and empathy for those on the margins of society—the sick, the poor, the outcasts. In Luke 5:12-13, Jesus heals a man with leprosy, touching him despite the social stigma attached to the disease. **[12] And it happened when He**

was in a certain city, that behold, a man who was full of leprosy saw Jesus; and he fell on *his* face and [b]implored Him, saying, "Lord, if You are willing, You can make me clean." [13] Then He put out *His* hand and touched him, saying, "I am willing; be cleansed." Immediately the leprosy left him. [14] And He charged him to tell no one, "But go and show yourself to the priest, and make an offering for your cleansing, as a testimony to them, just as Moses commanded."

2. **Forgiveness and Redemption:** Jesus exemplified forgiveness and redemption, offering grace and mercy to those who had sinned or fallen short. In John 8:1-11, Jesus forgives a woman caught in adultery, challenging her accusers to examine their own hearts and actions. **But Jesus went to the Mount of Olives.** [2] **Now [a]early in the morning He came again into the temple, and all the people came to Him; and He sat down and taught them.** [3] **Then the scribes and Pharisees brought to Him a woman caught in adultery. And when they had set her in the midst,** [4] **they said to Him, "Teacher, [b]this woman was caught in adultery, in the very act.** [5] **Now [c]Moses, in the law, commanded us [d]that such should be stoned. But what do You [e]say?"** [6] **This they said, testing Him, that they might have** *something* **of which to accuse Him. But Jesus stooped down and wrote on the ground with** *His* **finger, [f]as though He did not hear.** [7] **So when they continued asking Him, He [g]raised Himself up and said to them, "He who is without sin among you, let him throw a stone at her first."** [8] **And**

again He stooped down and wrote on the ground. [9] Then those who heard *it,* being[h] convicted by *their* conscience, went out one by one, beginning with the oldest *even* to the last. And Jesus was left alone, and the woman standing in the midst. [10] When Jesus had raised Himself up [i]and saw no one but the woman, He said to her, "Woman, where are those accusers [j]of yours? Has no one condemned you?" [11] She said, "No one, Lord." And Jesus said to her, "Neither do I condemn you; go [k]and sin no more."

3. **Servant Leadership:** Jesus embodied the essence of servant leadership, humbly serving others and prioritizing their needs above His own. In John 13:1-17, Jesus washes the feet of His disciples, even Judas, who He knew had already agreed to betray Him, demonstrating humility and servitude as the ultimate expression of love. (Acknowledge Steve Baumgartner) **Now before the Feast of the Passover, when Jesus knew that His hour had come that He should depart from this world to the Father, having loved His own who were in the world, He loved them to the end.**[2] **And** [a]**supper being ended, the devil having already put it into the heart of Judas Iscariot, Simon's** *son,* **to betray Him,** [3] **Jesus, knowing that the Father had given all things into His hands, and that He had come from God and was going to God,** [4] **rose from supper and laid aside His garments, took a towel and girded Himself.** [5] **After that, He poured water into a basin and began to wash the disciples' feet, and to wipe** *them* **with the towel with which He was girded.** [6] **Then He came to Simon**

Peter. And *Peter* said to Him, "Lord, are You washing my feet?" [7] Jesus answered and said to him, "What I am doing you do not understand now, but you will know after this." [8] Peter said to Him, "You shall never wash my feet!" Jesus answered him, "If I do not wash you, you have no part with Me." [9] Simon Peter said to Him, "Lord, not my feet only, but also *my* hands and *my* head!" [10] Jesus said to him, "He who is bathed needs only to wash *his* feet, but is completely clean; and you are clean, but not all of you." [11] For He knew who would betray Him; therefore He said, "You are not all clean." [12] So when He had washed their feet, taken His garments, and sat down again, He said to them, "Do you [b]know what I have done to you? [13] You call Me Teacher and Lord, and you say well, for *so* I am. [14] If I then, *your* Lord and Teacher, have washed your feet, you also ought to wash one another's feet. [15] For I have given you an example, that you should do as I have done to you. [16] Most assuredly, I say to you, a servant is not greater than his master; nor is he who is sent greater than he who sent him. [17] If you know these things, blessed are you if you do them.

4. **Selfless Sacrifice:** Jesus' willingness to sacrifice Himself for the salvation of humanity epitomizes the depth of His love. As stated in Philippians 2:5-8, Jesus humbled Himself, taking on the form of a servant and obediently accepting death on the cross for our sake. [5] Let this mind be in you which was also in Christ Jesus, [6] who, being in the form of God, did not consider

103

it [b]robbery to be equal with God, [7] but [c]made Himself of
no reputation, taking the form of a bondservant, *and* coming
in the likeness of men. [8] And being found in appearance as a
man, He humbled Himself and became obedient to *the point
of* death, even the death of the cross.

Jesus unequivocally commanded his followers to love their
neighbors as themselves. This commandment transcends social,
cultural, and economic boundaries, calling Christians to extend love
and compassion to all people, regardless of differences or
circumstances. **Mark 12:31 – "The second is this: 'Love your
neighbor as yourself.' There is no commandment greater than
these."**

In the Parable of the Good Samaritan, Jesus illustrated the
essence of loving one's neighbor through the selfless actions of a
Samaritan man who showed mercy to a wounded stranger,
transcending ethnic and religious barriers. Luke 10:25-37 – **"But a
Samaritan, as he traveled, came where the man was; and when
he saw him, he took pity on him. He went to him and bandaged
his wounds, pouring on oil and wine. Then he put the man on
his own donkey, brought him to an inn and took care of him."**

Jesus emphasized the importance of service as a defining
characteristic of his followers. He taught that true greatness comes
from serving others and encouraged his disciples to emulate his
example of servant leadership. Matthew 20:26-28 – **"Not so with
you. Instead, whoever wants to become great among you must
be your servant, and whoever wants to be first must be your**

slave—just as the Son of Man did not come to be served, but to serve, and to give his life as a ransom for many."

It is so important for believers to cultivate a servant's heart and start serving others. Three quick steps to get started are:

1. **Cultivating a Heart of Compassion:** Christians are called to cultivate a heart of compassion towards others, seeking to understand their needs and offer support and encouragement.

2. **Willingness to Sacrifice:** Following Jesus' example, Christians should be willing to sacrifice their own comfort, time, and resources for the well-being of others.

3. **Stepping Out of Comfort Zones:** True Christian service often requires stepping out of comfort zones and reaching out to those who are marginalized or in need.

The imperative for Christians to prepare themselves to serve others is deeply rooted in the life and teachings of Jesus Christ. The commandment to love our neighbor as ourselves serves as a guiding principle for Christian discipleship, compelling believers to embody the spirit of selflessness, compassion, and service in all aspects of their lives. As followers of Christ, let us heed his call to love and serve others, following his example of sacrificial love and humility.

Reflections:

The love that Christ had superseded his own safety, facing hostile crowds, healing a leper etc. What areas in your life have you sacrificed your comfort for others?

_____

_____

_____

How does the example of Jesus' forgiveness affect your own thoughts on forgiveness, acceptance, and love for those who may have a less-than-perfect past?

_____

_____

_____

In view of Jesus's love for even those who were looked down upon by society, how can we learn to accept our own as well as others' pasts? In light of the forgiveness we find at the foot of the cross, how should we accept others?

_____

_____

_____

Jesus' willingness to wash the feet of Judas, knowing of his betrayal, as well as the rest of the disciples, shows a willingness to not only serve others but to serve regardless of standing, treatment, or worth. What can we do to show the same commitment to the world around us?

_____

_____

_____

Prayer:

Dear Heavenly Father, help me to love like Jesus. Break my heart for those around me so that I can demonstrate Your love to all Your children. Let me overlook the slights and sins of others and focus on the value they have in You. Give me a servant's heart that loves to serve others and is always open and accepting of the opportunities You place before me. Amen

****In the next chapter, we look at a leader in the Old Testament who took the prompting of God seriously and led God's people to make a change and a difference. Nehemiah demonstrates what we, as Christ followers, need to replicate in order to take God's edict to the streets and LOVE OUR NEIGHBOR. ****

David Johnson

Chapter 10

Nehemiah's Example
Learning to Lead

~⟶●⟵~

Nehemiah was a Jewish cupbearer to King Artaxerxes I of Persia (465 B.C.- 424 B.C.), a position of significant trust and influence as he protected the King's life against poisoning every day. Although living in exile in Susa (modern-day Iran) and his high position, Nehemiah was deeply concerned about the plight of his people and the condition of Jerusalem, the city of his ancestors. Spurred by his love for God and his homeland, Nehemiah rose to the occasion, and God used him to bring a nation back to God.

In Nehemiah 1:1-4, Nehemiah learns from his brother Hanani and other men from Judah that Jerusalem's walls are broken down, and its gates are burned with fire. This news deeply disturbs Nehemiah, prompting him to weep, mourn, fast, and pray to God for several days. (1:5-11) Nehemiah prays, acknowledging God's greatness and faithfulness, confessing the sins of the Israelites, including his own and his father's house, and asking God to remember His promise to gather His people. Nehemiah then asks for success and favor as he plans to approach the king.

(2:1-8) Soon, Nehemiah draws the attention of the king as the heaviness of his heart in his presence causes concern, as it was unusual given his role. The king inquires about Nehemiah's sadness, and Nehemiah explains the distressing situation in Jerusalem. He then boldly requests permission to go to Jerusalem to rebuild it. King Artaxerxes grants Nehemiah's request and provides letters for safe passage and timber for construction. Nehemiah attributes this success to the gracious hand of God upon him. Not only did the king provide passage and his stature, but he also provided the material needed that ensure the work could be done. Nehemiah's boldness is rewarded.

In Nehemiah 2:11-16, we see Nehemiah arrive in Jerusalem, and after three days, he conducts a secret nighttime inspection of the walls to assess the damage and plan the reconstruction. He formulates a plan to repair the walls and rebuild not only Jerusalem but the faith of the nation. Soon (2:17-18), Nehemiah calls the Jewish leaders and the people together, sharing his vision and the support he has received from the king. He encourages them to start rebuilding, and they agree, saying, "Let us start rebuilding," and they begin the work with great enthusiasm.

Soon, opposition arises from Sanballat, the Horonite, Tobiah, the Ammonite official, and Geshem, the Arab. They mock and ridicule the Jews, accusing them of rebelling against the king and threatening attacks. Nehemiah responds with confidence in God's support and organizes the people to continue rebuilding despite the threats. He divides them into workers and armed guards, ensuring that construction continues while being prepared for potential attacks. It is said that they worked with one hand and held a sword in the other.

(6:15-16) Despite further plots and attempts to intimidate Nehemiah, he remains steadfast. The wall is completed in just 52 days, astonishing their enemies and demonstrating that God is faithful and has truly blessed the work that has been accomplished. Ezra, the scribe, reads the Law to the people, and they celebrate the Feast of Tabernacles. The people confess their sins and the sins of their ancestors, renewing their covenant with God.

Nehemiah continues to lead the people in reforms, ensuring the proper observance of the Law, restoring temple services, and addressing various social and religious issues. He reinforces the importance of keeping the Sabbath, supporting the Levites and temple workers, and maintaining the purity of the community by addressing intermarriage with foreigners. Not only did Nehemiah rebuild the walls, he also rebuilt the social, religious, and governance of the Jewish people—Returning the Israelites to their faith and cultural significance.

The story of Nehemiah is a powerful example of effective leadership, faith, and dedication. His ability to inspire and organize the people, his reliance on prayer and God's guidance, and his determination to overcome opposition and challenges provide timeless lessons for personal and community leadership. Nehemiah's commitment to justice, community, and faith underscores the importance of integrity and perseverance in achieving significant goals.

~

Nehemiah serves as a profound example of how dedicated leadership, faith, and a clear vision can mobilize a community to achieve significant and transformative goals. In today's world, Nehemiah may have started a nonprofit like Ben and Jess Owen, who traveled back to Memphis to rescue their adopted hometown from the violence and drug trade that was destroying it and nearly destroyed them, returning to rescue friends and take back Memphis house by house and block by block.

Or Scott Mann and his band of GWOT veterans (The Pineapple Express), who took up the cause of rescuing American allies left behind in our botched and badly handled withdrawal from Afghanistan. Joining together to rescue over a thousand people before the final plane left the ground and the country returned to the Taliban terrorists' control.

For the modern church, Nehemiah's journey offers invaluable lessons that can inspire and guide efforts to make a positive impact on the world. By examining Nehemiah's example, the church can find motivation and strategies to address contemporary challenges and serve as a beacon of hope and restoration in society.

First, Nehemiah's unwavering faith and reliance on prayer underscore the importance of spiritual grounding in any endeavor. Before taking action, Nehemiah sought God's guidance through fervent prayer, demonstrating his dependence on divine wisdom and strength. For the church, this highlights the necessity of rooting all missions and activities in prayer, seeking God's direction, and fostering a deep spiritual connection among its members. This foundation of faith ensures that the church's efforts are aligned with God's will and empowered by His grace, making them more effective and impactful.

Second, God uses unbelievers, the Government, and even those who are violently against our goals to accomplish His will. Learning to work with similarly aligned organizations, faith-based or not, greatly increases the ability and reach of our work, allowing those who may not know our savior or have animosity toward believers to see the love of Christ demonstrated in action and realize that everyone does not have to hold the same beliefs to achieve mutual goals. Judging those around you does nothing to advance the love of Christ and can greatly damage your witness to those around you.

Third, Nehemiah's vision to rebuild Jerusalem's walls illustrates the power of having a clear and compelling mission. His passionate commitment to this cause inspired others to join him, turning a daunting task into a collective effort. The church can draw from this by clearly articulating its vision for community service and social justice. By presenting a compelling and righteous cause, the church can galvanize its members and the broader secular community to work together towards common goals, such as alleviating poverty, fighting injustice, and providing support to the marginalized.

Fourth, Nehemiah's leadership in the face of opposition teaches the church about resilience and perseverance. Nehemiah encountered significant resistance from external enemies and internal challenges, yet he remained steadfast. He adapted his strategies, organized the people effectively, and encouraged them to stay focused despite the adversities. The church can learn from this resilience by preparing to face and overcome obstacles, whether they come in the form of societal opposition, resource constraints, or internal conflicts. Maintaining a steadfast commitment to its mission, the church can inspire confidence and determination within its community.

Fifth, Nehemiah's emphasis on community and unity is a powerful model for the church. He involved people from various backgrounds, assigning them tasks according to their skills, which fostered a sense of ownership and collaboration. This inclusivity and teamwork were crucial for the successful completion of the wall. The church can emulate this by fostering a strong sense of community, where every member feels valued and has a role to play. Encouraging volunteerism, leveraging diverse talents, and promoting unity can create a cohesive and motivated congregation capable of achieving remarkable feats.

Finally, Nehemiah's commitment to justice and social reform highlights the church's role in advocating for and enacting positive societal change. Nehemiah addressed the exploitation and injustices among his people, ensuring fairness and compassion prevailed. The church can follow this example by actively engaging in social justice initiatives, supporting the oppressed, and speaking out against injustices. By addressing the root causes of societal issues and providing practical assistance, the church can be a transformative force in the world, reflecting Christ's love and justice.

~

As God's church, what can we learn from the work Nehemiah did in rebuilding Jerusalem? We meet a successful professional, fully immersed in his career, seemingly at its peak. Yet, when he feels the movement of God, he doesn't hesitate. He sees a need, and instead of looking away, he steps forward—willing to sacrifice, to stake his reputation, and to take immense risks for people who have no direct connection to his life. We, as Christ's followers, should be willing to heed the same pulling at our spirit, following God's leadership to effect change and healing in a broken world.

Nehemiah exemplifies several admirable traits that we can aspire to exhibit in our own lives. Here are 10 traits based on Nehemiah's character and actions:

1. Leadership

- Nehemiah demonstrated strong leadership qualities by organizing and leading the rebuilding of Jerusalem's walls (Nehemiah 2:17-18).

2. Prayerfulness

- He was a man of prayer, seeking God's guidance and strength throughout his endeavors (Nehemiah 1:4-11; 2:4).

3. Courage

- Nehemiah displayed courage in the face of opposition and threats from enemies (Nehemiah 4:14).

4. Vision

- He had a clear vision and mission to rebuild the walls of Jerusalem, inspiring others to work towards a common goal. His deep concern for Jerusalem's condition drove his actions and decisions. (Nehemiah 2:17).

5. Perseverance

- Despite challenges, Nehemiah remained steadfast and persevered in his task, not giving in to discouragement or fear (Nehemiah 4:21-23).

6. Integrity

- Nehemiah maintained integrity in his leadership, refusing to exploit his position for personal gain or to oppress the people (Nehemiah 5:14-19).

7. Humility

- He demonstrated humility by acknowledging his dependence on God and his need for divine guidance and strength (Nehemiah 1:5-11).

8. Commitment to Justice

- Nehemiah was committed to justice and fairness, advocating for the rights and welfare of the people (Nehemiah 5:6-13).

9. Organizational Skills

- He exhibited strong organizational skills in planning and executing the rebuilding project effectively (Nehemiah 3:1-32).

10. Compassion

- Nehemiah showed compassion towards his people, empathizing with their hardships and actively working to alleviate their suffering (Nehemiah 1:3-4).

These traits from Nehemiah's life serve as powerful examples for us today, illustrating how faith, leadership, integrity, and compassion can shape our character and influence our actions in various aspects of life as we serve Christ by loving our neighbor and meeting their needs.

Leadership style, as depicted by Nehemiah, can be characterized by several key attributes and approaches that made him an effective leader. Here are the main aspects of Nehemiah's leadership style that can help us know how to fulfill God's lead.

1. Visionary Leadership

- **Proverbs 29:18: "Where there is no vision, the people perish; but happy is he who keeps the law."**

- **Habakkuk 2:2:** **"Then the Lord replied: 'Write down the revelation and make it plain on tablets so that a herald may run with it.'"**

Vision and Purpose:

- Nehemiah had a clear vision to rebuild the walls of Jerusalem and restore the city's dignity and safety. His deep concern for Jerusalem's condition drove his actions and decisions.

- He communicated this vision effectively to the people, inspiring them to participate in the rebuilding efforts.

Application Today:

- Personal Goals: Just as Nehemiah had a clear vision to rebuild Jerusalem, individuals today can benefit from having clear, purposeful goals in their personal and professional lives.

- Organizational Vision: Leaders in organizations and communities can articulate a clear vision to inspire and unite people toward a common goal.

2. Prayerful and Spiritual Leadership

- **Philippians 4:6-7:** **"Do not be anxious about anything, but in every situation, by prayer and petition, with thanksgiving, present your requests to God. And the peace of God, which transcends all understanding, will guard your hearts and your minds in Christ Jesus."**

- **Proverbs 3:5-6: "Trust in the Lord with all your heart and lean not on your own understanding; in all your ways submit to him, and he will make your paths straight."**

Dependence on Prayer:

- Nehemiah consistently sought God's guidance and support through prayer. Before taking any significant action, he prayed for wisdom, strength, and favor.

- His prayers were not just personal but also communal, seeking God's intervention for the well-being of the people and the success of the project.

Application Today:

- Personal Faith: Nehemiah's reliance on prayer highlights the importance of seeking spiritual guidance and strength. Individuals can incorporate regular prayer or meditation into their daily routines for guidance and support.

- Community Faith: Encouraging a culture of prayer or spiritual reflection within organizations and communities can help maintain a sense of purpose and resilience.

3. Strategic and Practical Leadership

- **1 Peter 4:10: "Each of you should use whatever gift you have received to serve others, as faithful stewards of God's grace in its various forms."**

- Romans 12:6-8: "We have different gifts, according to the grace given to each of us. If your gift is prophesying, then prophesy in accordance with your faith; if it is serving, then serve; if it is teaching, then teach; if it is to encourage, then give encouragement; if it is giving, then give generously; if it is to lead, do it diligently; if it is to show mercy, do it cheerfully."

Planning and Organization:

- Nehemiah was a strategic planner. He carefully assessed the situation, made detailed plans, and allocated resources effectively.

- He organized the work by assigning specific sections of the wall to different groups, ensuring that the workload was distributed and manageable.

Application Today:

- Goal Setting: Nehemiah's strategic approach to rebuilding the walls can be applied to personal and professional project planning. Setting clear objectives, assessing resources, and creating detailed plans are essential for success.

- Resource Management: Effective allocation and management of resources, as demonstrated by Nehemiah, are crucial for the success of any project or initiative.

4. Motivational Leadership

- James 2:15-16: "Suppose a brother or a sister is without clothes and daily food. If one of you says to them, 'Go in peace;

keep warm and well fed,' but does nothing about their physical needs, what good is it?"

- Isaiah 58:10: "And if you spend yourselves in behalf of the hungry and satisfy the needs of the oppressed, then your light will rise in the darkness, and your night will become like the noonday."

Inspiring and Encouraging:

- Nehemiah motivated the people by sharing his vision and showing unwavering commitment to the task. His passion and dedication inspired others to join and stay committed to the work.

- He encouraged the workers, addressed their fears, and provided the moral support needed to overcome obstacles and opposition.

Application Today:

- Inspiration: Leaders can inspire their teams by sharing a compelling vision and demonstrating commitment and passion. Nehemiah's ability to motivate and encourage his people is a model for effective leadership.

- Encouragement: Regularly encouraging and supporting team members can boost morale and productivity.

5. Resilient and Courageous Leadership

- Romans 5:3-4: "Not only so, but we also glory in our sufferings, because we know that suffering produces perseverance; perseverance, character; and character, hope."

- James 1:2-4: "Consider it pure joy, my brothers and sisters, whenever you face trials of many kinds, because you know that the testing of your faith produces perseverance. Let perseverance finish its work so that you may be mature and complete, not lacking anything."

Facing Opposition:

- Nehemiah demonstrated resilience and courage in the face of significant opposition from external enemies and internal challenges. He remained steadfast in his mission despite threats and attempts to discourage him.

- He took practical steps to protect the workers, such as organizing armed guards and encouraging the people to be vigilant.

Application Today:

- Overcoming Challenges: Nehemiah's resilience in the face of opposition teaches the importance of perseverance. Individuals and organizations should be prepared to face challenges and remain steadfast in their efforts.

- Adaptability: Adapting strategies to overcome obstacles, as Nehemiah did, is crucial in today's rapidly changing world.

6. Servant Leadership

Psalm 133:1: "How good and pleasant it is when God's people live together in unity!"

1 Corinthians 12:12-14: "Just as a body, though one, has many parts, but all its many parts form one body, so it is with Christ."

Leading by Example:

- Nehemiah led by example, showing humility and a servant's heart. He worked alongside the people, shared in their struggles, and did not exploit his position for personal gain.

- He was committed to the well-being of the people, addressing their grievances, and ensuring justice and fairness, especially when dealing with issues like debt and exploitation.

Application Today:

- Leading by Example: Leaders can follow Nehemiah's example of servant leadership by working alongside their teams and prioritizing the well-being of their people.

- Ethical Leadership: Maintaining integrity, fairness, and justice in leadership decisions fosters trust and respect.

7. Collaborative and Inclusive Leadership

Psalm 133:1: "How good and pleasant it is when God's people live together in unity!"

- 1 Corinthians 12:12-14: "Just as a body, though one, has many parts, but all its many parts form one body, so it is with Christ."

Building Team Spirit:

- Nehemiah fostered a sense of community and teamwork. He involved various groups, including priests, nobles, and common people, in the rebuilding process.

- By recognizing and valuing each person's contribution, he created a united front that was crucial for the project's success.

Application Today:

- Teamwork: Nehemiah's ability to unite people from different backgrounds to work towards a common goal underscores the power of teamwork and collaboration.

- Community Engagement: Engaging and involving the community in decision-making processes can lead to more effective and inclusive outcomes.

Nehemiah's leadership style was a blend of visionary, prayerful, strategic, motivational, resilient, servant, and collaborative leadership. His ability to inspire, organize, and persevere, combined with his deep faith and commitment to his mission, made him an effective and respected leader. Nehemiah's story provides valuable lessons in leadership that are applicable in various contexts, emphasizing the importance of vision, prayer, strategic planning, motivation, resilience, servant leadership, and collaboration.

Taking the lessons learned from Nehemiah, we can begin to lead efforts, build momentum, and inspire others to follow as we begin the task of loving our neighbors. Following God's will for our communities, churches, and families, we can make a difference by applying what we learned and being the change our world needs.

Begin the search today, get alone with God and let Him speak to your heart to break it for those around us who have no hope and need help physically. Because until we meet the basic needs of the body, we will have a tough time reaching them for their eternal needs.

Reflections:

How can we use the example of Nehemiah to learn to create avenues to serve others?

_____

_____

_____

How can we apply the direction of work and willingness to fight in our desire to help others?

_____

_____

_____

When faced with seemingly insurmountable opposition, even from fellow believers, how can we build bridges that bring differing worlds together?

_____

_____

_____

Is it acceptable to use secular organizations to achieve the goals that God put before us? If not, is the use of Government funds acceptable? In the case of Nehemiah, God used the King to advance His calling; how does this affect your views?

_____

_____

_____

How can we use secular organizations without sacrificing our ultimate goal of leading others to Christ? Knowing that we must first reach the physical, how do we also serve the spiritual opportunities presented?

_____

_____

_____

Prayer:

Dear Heavenly Father, strengthen my resolve to help others. Give me the faith and courage to stand up for the marginalized, the looked down upon, the unfavored, and the least of Your children. I pray for courage in the face of criticism for aligning with those who don't look like me or believe like me, but nonetheless, have worth like me. Help me to look for the unbeliever that You may put in my way to further Your cause and live an example of Your love before them at every opportunity. Amen

Chapter 11

Build your Ark

———————————⌒◉⌒———————————

W hen a Christian dies, the only question that matters is, "Did you do what you were supposed to do?" Did you build your ark? Fight your giant? Wrestle your lion? Just as Nehemiah found his calling to rebuild Jerusalem, we must find our calling and purpose in Christ Jesus.

In faith, Noah built an ark. Out of faith, he built something that he had no use for. He lived in the desert and never even saw rain, so he had no frame of reference for any type of floating device, much less a ship over a football field long. A ship that was not matched until centuries later.

Yet Noah, in faith, did as God commanded him—Ignored the stares, the smirks, the ridicule to follow God's leading.

For 100 years, Noah faithfully worked on the ark. Jewish tradition even says he grew the trees needed for the ark. Can you even fathom that kind of faith that you wait 20 years just for the material to start the process of building the vision God gave you?

And then he spent over a year locked in a boat that God sealed shut, and faithfully cared for the animals God put in his care.

That kind of faith is not looking for recognition; it is keeping your head down, eyes on the task, and shoulder-to-the-wheel kind of faith. It aims to please God, not fit the world narrative.

So, the story of Noah should make us ask ourselves a few questions. What is your purpose? What have you been called to do? Are you fulfilling God's purpose in your life?

I worked for my dad as a young man and enjoyed all the security that entailed, but when he retired, I had to choose a path that did not contain the same security and safety net. I had to make a choice, hatch a plan, put together a roadmap to secure myself and my family's future, and I did. I put together a five-year plan that entailed finishing my degree, getting into a position with upward mobility, and working my tail off to get into a middle management position in less than 5 years.

I was focused on finishing my degree while working long hours. At one time, I worked 2 full-time jobs to make sure I landed in a position of leadership. At the 4-year mark, I was hired into a management training program that provided everything I had been hoping for and was a springboard to leadership lessons, personal growth, and financial stability that I had been working toward.

Working without a net, outside my comfort zone, and in industries I knew nothing about tested my faith and resolve. But with a great wife backing me and a faith that God had blessed this route and had opened these doors, I succeeded. If I had not trusted that God had a plan, loved me, and wanted me to trust His way, I never would have gone far beyond my abilities to a place He had for me.

And now, years into my path, I can look back and see how God pushed, moved, forced, and guided my path. How one step built on another, how a setback became a huge step forward, and how my faith and willingness to leap where He directed led to great things for my whole family.

You see, most of us go to the point of precedence and fail to go into the unknown. We refuse to forge ahead where we have never been before, instead opting to stay within the confines of what has been. By doing so, we leave new experiences, blessings, and treasures for someone else to discover.

The old saying goes, if you keep doing what you've been doing, you will keep getting what you have been getting. In order to change your life and meet your destiny, you must step out of your comfort zone.

Dare to fail. Dare to fail BIG. Dare to fail boldly!

Because it will give you experience, knowledge, and wisdom. Because failure builds character in those who do not give up but stand back up, dust themselves off, and move forward.

Do not be ashamed of audacious goals. Don't let self-doubt or imposter syndrome hold you back. Trust that what God put in your heart is within your abilities, even if you don't possess them today.

My first leadership position was as a softball coach. I was not the most talented on the team, but I knew the game, how to structure a batting order, and recruit the best guys. I didn't let my lesser talent keep me from building a winning team that traveled and competed with anybody. I knew my strengths and played to them. On this team, I wasn't the shortstop or 4th batter, but I filled my role and coached a great team.

Live your passions, and follow the path God is showing you. Prayerfully ask for the guts, the will, and the resolve to do the thing God has put in your soul.

God is calling you to obey. You may serve His purpose in your failure rather than in your success. Your task may just be to move someone else into action, not actually solve the problem.

You may always be the one planting the seed and never see the harvest. You may live your life thinking that you were not successful, only to arrive in heaven to vast treasures. Trust the moving of the Lord in your life.

There comes a time when we must stop making excuses and build our ark!

Moses felt ridiculous demanding Pharaoh let God's people go with nothing to back it up. Until—Pharaoh freed the Israelites, and they left with the gold and silver given to them by the Egyptians

The children of Israel probably felt foolish marching around Jericho playing trumpets. Until—the walls of Jericho fell before their eyes, and the city was theirs.

David was probably nervous as he faced a giant with three smooth stones. Until—a giant fell dead at his feet, and the Philistines were routed.

Joseph pushed down his shame to trust that Mary was indeed carrying the Messiah. Until—Jesus rose from the dead and saved humanity.

Peter was scared to death, and the other Disciples stayed in the boat as he stepped out of the boat and into the water. Until—his first step held him above the waves.

Naaman had to be rebuked by his servant to wash himself 7 times in muddy waters as the prophet instructed. Until—he rose the seventh time, cleansed of his leprosy.

Until is a five-letter word that separates faith from reason. Indecision from action. Belief from doubt.

God wants us to be a vessel for His glorification.

He wants us to be able to say, as Paul did, "The time for my departure is near. [7] I have fought the good fight, I have finished the race, I have kept the faith. [8] Now there is in store for me the crown of righteousness, which the Lord, the righteous Judge, will award to me on that day." 2 Timothy 4: 6-8

God does not need us, but praise God, He uses us in His Plan, allowing us to share in the Glory of His plan. We need to make our hearts ready to be used—Steel our resolve to be a vessel to be used for the furtherance of His Gospel.

Right now, we see the terror, the evil and the gross sin that has become the norm in our world. The brokenness around us in our homes, communities, and world that God is calling us to take a stand against. To be different, to stand out like that light on the hill or the salt that flavors all it touches.

We need to faithfully build the ark that God is calling us to build, regardless of the looks, ridicule, or persecution from the world.

We should live our lives not for the adoration of the world, or acclaim or notoriety, but for the applause from hands scarred by nails.

Reflections

Has God burdened your heart with certain people, problems, or ministry? What have you done about it?

_____

_____

_____

What gifts do you have that God can use? What experience has He given you to prepare you to fight for others, win the battle, and set His people free?

_____

_____

_____

What issues do you see around you that burden your heart, that you have skills that could be useful in helping, or contacts that could promote their solution?

_____

_____

_____

List 5 skills that you possess that would be useful in God's service.

1.

2.

3.

4.

5.

List 5 problems, issues, or burdens that burden your heart.

1.

2.

3.

4.

5.

Spend time in prayer for God's leading in what He would have you do to use these gifts to solve these problems. Pray for guidance, opportunity, and faith to step into the gap that He reveals for you.

Prayer:

Lord, reveal to us our purpose in Your plan. Open our eyes to see Your children the way You do so that we can be Your hands and feet in this world. Gives us the faith of Noah, the fearlessness of David, the vision of Nehemiah, and the obedience of Joshua at the battle of Jericho. Awaken our hearts, burden our souls, and provide opportunity to serve You by loving our neighbor. Amen

Chapter 12

We Don't Set the Pace

———————⌒⌒●⌒⌒———————

From the Streets to Heaven

As we go to the mission field to save, serve, and satisfy the needs of the hurting and abused, we need to recognize our role not only in the short game but in the long game as well. Leading a conversation with someone who has no food with "If you died tonight, would you go to heaven?" will gain you no more than a blank stare and bewilderment. WE MUST meet the physical needs first before we have the credibility to talk about eternity. But once we have met and satisfied the basic needs and the physical person is safe, we need to be prepared for a conversation about eternity.

Understanding that we cannot force the conversation, we need to be patient. Without knowing someone's history with faith or religion, we stand the chance of walking into a minefield filled with disappointments, judgment, and hurt that could blow up and break our credibility. While some will readily move into faith, others will have had experiences that make them hesitant or downright hostile to God's word. We can only exhibit the love of Christ in hopes that they will be moved to trust us enough to hear. But scars run deep, and some things only God can heal.

Trusting that the Holy Spirit will use our efforts to open the door for a saving conversation is oftentimes hard, as we want to hurry up the process. But we must realize that God is in control, and although we must be ready, available, and willing, God's time is what will drive their heart. Waiting on the prompting of the Holy Spirit is our job, and we must be ready.

Steps to Personal Salvation

Realizing the Need

Recognizing that we are in need of saving is the first and most pivotal step a person must take in order to meet God. Without the realization that our own nature and God-given free will put us at odds with our creator, there can be no true relationship. Just as if you failed to recognize the need to breathe, you would eventually suffer the effects of no oxygen and pass out. Hopefully, you were not underwater at the time because once you passed out, your own body would recognize the need and involuntarily gasp for air.

In the same way, our body recognizes our physical needs, our spirit recognizes our spiritual needs. I truly believe that we are all born with a God-sized hole in our lives that only He can fill. Psalm 42:1-2 (NIV): **"As the deer pants for streams of water, so my soul pants for you, my God. My soul thirsts for God, for the living God. When can I go and meet with God?"** Many of us spend a lifetime trying to fill that hole with drugs, people, money, status, or activities to no avail. Often, we realize too late what our spirit is yearning for, or worse yet, fail to ever come to the point of realization that our spirit longs for our creator, our Father.

Romans 3:23 says, **"For all have sinned and fall short of the glory of God,"** which means that there is no one who is without sin; we call this the universality of sin. As Adam sinned in the garden, he introduced sin into the whole world, and since every one of us is from the lineage of Adam, we have the same sin curse as him. Romans 5:12**: "Therefore, just as sin came into the world through one man, and death through sin, and so death spread to all men because all sinned."** We have no desire within our hearts to repent, and without the drawing of the Holy Spirit, we will remain stubborn and selfish in our ways, depending upon our own abilities to secure our eternity. Galatians 5:17 says, **"For the desires of the flesh are against the Spirit, and the desires of the Spirit are against the flesh, for these are opposed to each other, to keep you from doing the things you want to do."** We as Christians have come to realize our need through the prompting of the Holy Spirit, and we must rely on His prompting for those we seek to help.

Prayer is our response to a hardened heart and someone who does not seem to want to discuss eternal things. The Bible tells us that fervent prayer produces results. God will soften the heart, and it is up to that person to react with regret and sorrow for the sin that is in their life. When that time comes, there will be obvious questions and seeking that we need to be prepared for.

The next step – Repentance and turning from sin

True repentance involves a heartfelt acknowledgment of one's sins, a sincere turning away from those sins, and a commitment to live a transformed life in obedience to God. It's the same idea as if you are on a road trip and suddenly realize you are heading south on the interstate when you should be heading north. You find the first opportunity to turn around and head in the opposite direction. Repentance looks exactly the same: the realization that the path you are on is not leading to the place you want to be, and you turn 180 degrees and head toward Jesus.

Recognition without repentance is just the opposite. You realize you are heading in the wrong direction, but as you come to the first exit, you doubt your directions or your destination and decide to see where this path leads. You end up lost or in a place that is not where you want to be, costing precious time, money, and opportunity that you may not get back.

Several scriptures provide a comprehensive view of what true repentance looks like:

1. Confession and Recognition of Sin:

1 John 1:9: **"If we confess our sins, he is faithful and just and will forgive us our sins and purify us from all unrighteousness."**

2. Godly Sorrow and Regret:

2 Corinthians 7:10: **"Godly sorrow brings repentance that leads to salvation and leaves no regret, but worldly sorrow brings death."**

3. Turning Away from Sin:

Acts 3:19**: "Repent, then, and turn to God, so that your sins may be wiped out, that times of refreshing may come from the Lord."**

4. Change in Behavior and Deeds:

Matthew 3:8: **"Produce fruit in keeping with repentance."**

Acts 26:20: **"First to those in Damascus, then to those in Jerusalem and in all Judea, and then to the Gentiles, I preached that they should repent and turn to God and demonstrate their repentance by their deeds."**

5. Seeking Forgiveness and Restoration:

Luke 15:10: **"In the same way, I tell you, there is rejoicing in the presence of the angels of God over one sinner who repents."**

6. Commitment to Follow God:

Romans 12:1-2: **"Therefore, I urge you, brothers and sisters, in view of God's mercy, to offer your bodies as a living sacrifice, holy and pleasing to God—this is your true and proper worship. Do not conform to the pattern of this world but be transformed by the renewing of your mind. Then you will be able to test and approve what God's will is—his good, pleasing and perfect will."**

Galatians 5:24**: "Those who belong to Christ Jesus have crucified the flesh with its passions and desires."**

True repentance, therefore, is not merely feeling sorry for sin but involves a comprehensive change in heart, mind, and behavior. It is characterized by confession, genuine remorse, turning away from sin, and a steadfast commitment to follow God and live according to His will.

Results of Repentance

Regeneration refers to the spiritual rebirth or renewal of a person. It is a transformative process brought about by the Holy Spirit, in which a person is made spiritually alive and given a new nature in Christ. This concept is closely tied to salvation and becoming a new creation in Christ. Here are key aspects of regeneration with supporting scriptures:

1. Spiritual Rebirth:

John 3:3-7: **"Jesus replied, 'Very truly I tell you, no one can see the kingdom of God unless they are born again.' 'How can someone be born when they are old?' Nicodemus asked. 'Surely they cannot enter a second time into their mother's womb to be born!' Jesus answered, 'Very truly I tell you, no one can enter the kingdom of God unless they are born of water and the Spirit. Flesh gives birth to flesh, but the Spirit gives birth to spirit. You should not be surprised at my saying, 'You must be born again.'"**

2. New Creation:

2 Corinthians 5:17: **"Therefore, if anyone is in Christ, the new creation has come: The old has gone, the new is here!"**

Galatians 6:15: **"Neither circumcision nor uncircumcision means anything; what counts is the new creation."**

3. Transformation by the Holy Spirit:

Titus 3:5: **"He saved us, not because of righteous things we had done, but because of his mercy. He saved us through the washing of rebirth and renewal by the Holy Spirit."**

Ezekiel 36:26-27: **"I will give you a new heart and put a new spirit in you; I will remove from you your heart of stone and give you a heart of flesh. And I will put my Spirit in you and move you to follow my decrees and be careful to keep my laws."**

4. Adoption as Children of God:

John 1:12-13: **"Yet to all who did receive him, to those who believed in his name, he gave the right to become children of God—children born not of natural descent, nor of human decision or a husband's will, but born of God."**

Romans 8:15-16: **"The Spirit you received does not make you slaves so that you live in fear again; rather, the Spirit you received brought about your adoption to sonship. And by him, we cry, 'Abba, Father.' The Spirit himself testifies with our spirit that we are God's children."**

5. Eternal Life:

1 Peter 1:23: **"For you have been born again, not of perishable seed, but of imperishable, through the living and enduring word of God."**

John 10:28-29: **"I give them eternal life, and they shall never perish; no one will snatch them out of my hand. My Father, who has given them to me, is greater than all; no one can snatch them out of my Father's hand."**

6. Living a New Life:

Romans 6:4: **"We were therefore buried with him through baptism into death in order that, just as Christ was raised from the dead through the glory of the Father, we too may live a new life."**

Colossians 3:9-10: **"Do not lie to each other, since you have taken off your old self with its practices and have put on the new self, which is being renewed in knowledge in the image of its Creator."**

Regeneration, therefore, signifies a profound and divine change in a person's life. It involves being born again through the Holy Spirit, becoming a new creation, and being adopted as children of God, all of which result in living a transformed life that aligns with God's will.

Significance of the adoption

I want to share more with you on the transformative truth of our adoption into the family of God, a theme that is beautifully woven throughout the New Testament. This concept not only defines our identity as believers but also reshapes our understanding of our relationship with God and each other.

First, God chose us before the creation of the world.

Ephesians 1:4-5: **"For he chose us in him before the creation of the world to be holy and blameless in his sight. In love, he predestined us for adoption to sonship through Jesus Christ, in accordance with his pleasure and will."**

Second, He made a way for us to come to Him by sending His Son.

John 1:12-13: **"Yet to all who did receive him, to those who believed in his name, he gave the right to become children of God, children born not of natural descent, nor of human decision or a husband's will, but born of God."**

Third, to understand the depth of His love for us, it is to understand how He looks at us.

Romans 8:14-17: **"For those who are led by the Spirit of God are the children of God. The Spirit you received does not make you slaves, so that you live in fear again; rather, the Spirit you received brought about your adoption to sonship. And by him we cry, 'Abba, Father.' The Spirit himself testifies with our spirit that we are God's children. Now if we are children, then we are heirs—heirs of God and co-heirs with Christ, if indeed we share in his sufferings in order that we may also share in his glory."**

By law, it is harder to disavow an adopted child than a birth child. And although we love our children with all our hearts, the fact that we actually choose the adopted child adds weight to the value we put on them. This passage reveals several key aspects of our divine adoption. First, it tells us that being led by the Spirit of God confirms our identity as His children. This is not a superficial change but a profound transformation that frees us from the bondage of fear and sin. The Spirit we receive brings us into an intimate relationship with God, enabling us to call Him "Abba, Father," a term of deep affection and trust.

Paul goes on in Galatians 4:4-7: **"God sent his Son, born of a woman, born under the law, to redeem those under the law, that we might receive adoption to sonship. Because you are his sons, God sent the Spirit of his Son into our hearts, the Spirit who calls out, 'Abba, Father.' So you are no longer a slave, but God's child; and since you are his child, God has made you also an heir."**

Here, we see that our adoption is rooted in the redemptive work of Jesus Christ. Through His life, death, and resurrection, Jesus made it possible for us to be adopted into God's family. This adoption changes our status from slaves to children and heirs. As heirs, we have a glorious inheritance, not just in the life to come but also in our current relationship with God, where we can experience His love, guidance, and presence daily.

Ephesians 1:4-5 further deepens our understanding: **"For he chose us in him before the creation of the world to be holy and blameless in his sight. In love he predestined us for adoption to sonship through Jesus Christ, in accordance with his pleasure and will."**

These verses remind us that our adoption was part of God's eternal plan. It was not an afterthought but a deliberate act of love and grace. God chose us to be His children before the foundation of the world, underscoring the depth of His love and the intentionality of His plan for us.

In John 1:12-13, we read, **"Yet to all who did receive him, to those who believed in his name, he gave the right to become children of God, children born not of natural descent, nor of human decision or a husband's will, but born of God."**

This passage highlights that our adoption into God's family is a gift given to all who receive and believe in Jesus. It's a new birth, not based on human effort or lineage but on the divine will and power of God. This new birth grants us the right to be called children of God, affirming our new identity and status.

Securing the adoption;

• 1 John 1:9: **"If we confess our sins, he is faithful and just to forgive us our sins and to cleanse us from all unrighteousness."**

• Ephesians 1:7: **"In him we have redemption through his blood, the forgiveness of our trespasses, according to the riches of his grace."**

The breadth of His forgiveness:

• Psalm 103:12: **"As far as the east is from the west, so far does he remove our transgressions from us."**

• Colossians 1:13-14: **"He has delivered us from the domain of darkness and transferred us to the kingdom of his beloved Son, in whom we have redemption, the forgiveness of sins."**

Ephesians 3:17-19: **"And I pray that you, being rooted and established in love, may have power…. to grasp how wide and long and high and deep is the love of Christ, and to know this love that surpasses knowledge."**

As His children, we are set apart and no longer citizens of this world. We are now strangers in a strange land. With different priorities and different objectives. 1 John 3:1 says, **"See what great love the Father has lavished on us, that we should be called children of God! And that is what we are! The reason the world does not know us is that it did not know him."**

The relationship of the believer in Christ with our Father encompasses repentance, redemption, forgiveness, and adoption. Repentance is the recognition of our depravity and need for God to redeem us and bring us to Him. Redemption is the deliverance from sin and death through Jesus' sacrifice. Forgiveness is the complete pardon of sins granted through faith in Christ. Adoption is the act of being made children of God, securing a new identity and intimate relationship with Him. Together, these aspects highlight the fullness of salvation offered to believers, transforming their lives and restoring their relationship with God.

Reflections:

Does waiting on God to work in the heart of an unbeliever fit with your personal style of witnessing? Are you comfortable with showing up in love and waiting on the prompting of the Holy Spirit?

_____

_____

_____

Do you currently feel comfortable answering questions from someone seeking answers about eternity? What scriptures would you use?

_____

_____

_____

When thinking of God as our Father, what attributes come to mind, and how does this affect your faith?

_____

_____

_____

How does the thought of being adopted into God's family make you feel about your personal relationship with God?

_____

_____

_____

If someone asked you, "How do you know that there is a heaven?" what would you say?

_____

_____

_____

If their second question was, "How can you know you are going there?" What would you say?

_____

_____

_____

When someone says, "I've been a good person, of course, I'm going to heaven," what do you say?'

_____

_____

_____

Prayer:
Dear heavenly Father, teach me the right way to lead others to
You. Let my life reflect Your love, and my words edify You. Never
let my desire for an outcome get in the way of Your work. Lead
me and guide me as I tell others about You. Amen

David Johnson

Chapter 13

Now we go

————————⌒◉⌒————————

W hen Jesus asked the people, "Who was a neighbor to the man beside the road?" they replied, "He who showed mercy on him."

Jesus' response to the crowd was simply, **"Go and do likewise."**

Go and do likewise. Jesus has laid out before us in verse after verse in the Bible what He would have us do—Serve others. It is so simple and direct that we cannot miss it. If we can't miss it, then we must be in willful disobedience of our Lord.

Jesus told Peter to FEED MY SHEEP, so we built a Starbucks in the lobby.

All around us, people outside the church are starting nonprofits and ministries to fill the gap left by our modern-day church. Because Christians refuse to step up and help the hungry, hurting and desperate where they are, others have stepped into the void.

Helping others has become a business that can often be wasteful and sometimes actually corrupt. Larger nonprofits using the name of Christ or religion have blackened the eye of the charitable space and have made it impossible to trust that your money is actually helping.

Because of survivors who saw the corruption of the systems, there are grassroots organizations that are popping up across our nation to go back and help those who are left in the gutters and streets of our nation.

A CALL TO RETURN TO OUR MISSION

This book attempts to call the Church, each and every Christ follower, to do as Christ commanded and love our neighbor. Find a place to help others, a cause that relieves the suffering of your neighbor, and a calling that will allow you the privilege to serve our Lord.

Whether it is:

Working with the addicted

The sex trafficked and abused

The hungry and poor

Protecting our children

Protecting our nation

Protecting our streets

Righting wrongs

Find your passion, what God has put on your heart, and go serve. There are people scattered all over this country who have built processes, foundations and frameworks that need your help to continue helping others.

We must forge alliances that open avenues to help the lost and dying in our world. Look across lines that often separate us from secular organizations whose goals are aligned with ours, but who distrust formal religion because of past experiences or misguided ideas. The analogy that Scott used was his very real experience gaining the trust of Afghan villagers who had every reason not to trust his Green Beret team. But by coming along beside them and fighting a common enemy, risking their own lives, they built bridges to effect change. Why can't the church do the same?

Scott says, "Relationships are strategic assets. Social capital is at the heart of how people, teammates, employers, and clients take action. Social capital is comprised of the tangible and intangible linkages between you and other people. Rapport. Loyalty. Reciprocity. You get the idea." As the church, we need to create a symbiotic relationship with sometimes secular groups to reach and address the hurting, meeting basic physical needs, so that we can be trusted with the more important spiritual needs at a later date.

We do not set God's timing or do the saving. We need to trust that doing what God instructed us to do—love our Neighbors—will open our hearts to God's leading and lead to the salvation of the whole person.

In the next section, I want to highlight Heroes who are doing great work. Men and women deserve to be recognized for their work and willingness to address the wrongs they saw, the needs they witnessed, or the dangers facing our society. These heroes deserve to be recognized as they sacrifice their time, their finances, and sometimes their safety to serve their fellow man to love their neighbor.

In the following section, I want to recognize several nonprofits that deserve your help. Each is carrying much of the weight themselves and could use partners to help carry the load. As you read through these great organizations, I challenge you to find one or two that speak to your heart and, if feasible, give your time and, if not, commit a monthly gift that will take the love of God to the hurting and dying world.

Remember that when Jesus was asked what the greatest commandment was, He said in Mark 12:29-31, **"The first of all the commandments is: 'Hear, O Israel, the Lord our God, the Lord is one. 30 And you shall love the Lord your God with all your heart, with all your soul, with all your mind, and with all your strength.' [l]This is the first commandment. 31 And the second, like it, is this: 'You shall love your neighbor as yourself.' There is no other commandment greater than these."** As His church, I implore each of us to obey and begin today to serve and love our neighbor.

Prayer:

Dear Heavenly Father, use me. Help me to realize that Your commandment should shape my life, my actions, and the way I see Your children. Take away self, and help me to focus on the needs around me. Help me to retain my first love and to never take what You have done for me for granted. Help me remember what I was before You saved me, and always strive to be worthy of Your love by loving others. Help me to be a Neighbor to everyone I meet. Amen.

Non-Profit Organizations

Doing God's Work

In a world where government policies falter, religious institutions waver, and society turns a blind eye to the suffering of its most vulnerable, nonprofit organizations have emerged as lifelines for the forgotten. While political leaders debate and faith communities struggle with their own internal conflicts, these grassroots organizations quietly step in, offering food, shelter, medical care, and hope to those abandoned by the very systems meant to protect them. Their work is not driven by profit, power, or public recognition but by a deep, unshakable belief in humanity's responsibility to care for one another.

For generations, the church and the community met the needs of the hurting, but beginning in the last century, many began placing their trust in government programs to provide a safety net for their needs. Yet, time and time again, bureaucratic red tape, shifting priorities, and budget cuts have left millions without essential resources. Likewise, religious institutions, once the moral compass of communities, found themselves entangled in ideological battles rather than standing firm in their mission to serve the poor and marginalized. And society at large, consumed with consumerism and self-interest, has largely chosen indifference over action. It is within this void that nonprofits rise, embodying the compassion, urgency, and effectiveness that other institutions have neglected.

These organizations do more than just provide immediate relief; they advocate, innovate, and challenge the status quo. They build sustainable solutions where governments fail to act, create safe spaces where churches have excluded, and extend dignity where society has cast shame. From food banks and housing initiatives to healthcare access and legal advocacy, nonprofits are tackling the issues others deem too complex or inconvenient. They are run by individuals who refuse to accept the status quo—people who see a broken system and dare to mend it with whatever resources they can muster.

This section of the book highlights some of the extraordinary organizations that labor tirelessly in the shadows to bring light to the most neglected corners of our world. Their work is not a substitute for what governments and churches should be doing but rather a testament to what happens when ordinary individuals refuse to wait for permission to do what is right. There are far too many to mention, and this list by no means is all encompassing, but are men and women that I know personally and could use your support.

In the face of institutional failure, nonprofits have proven that compassion and action can still thrive. They remind us that change is possible—not through bureaucracy or empty promises, but through the hands and hearts of those willing to step forward. Their existence is a call to action, a reminder that we, too, can be part of the solution. The question is: Where do you fit? Will you answer that call?

Whether it is helping underprivileged kids in the worst neighborhoods get a hand up and out of poverty by exposing them to military and law enforcement opportunities or providing job training and life skills to those in desperate need of new perspectives, some of these nonprofits are helping the poorest among us see a life they never saw before.

Others are providing protection, training, and technology to disrupt and arrest those involved in child pornography, abuse, and trafficking. By using their gifts and passion, they are rescuing and protecting children who are experiencing things that they should never have to endure. The men and women who are giving their time in places that most can't even imagine are often traumatized by what they see and experience.

Still, others are going into the streets where drugs are ruining lives, tearing apart families, and killing our youth in record numbers, offering opportunities for recovery, a loving embrace, or just a warm bed to those in the throes of addiction, rescuing women from the streets and their traffickers where they are degraded and used in inhumane ways, kept in addiction by those who often claim to be their protectors.

There are so many needs and so few volunteers. These organizations welcome your inquiries, donations and offers of help as they stand in the gap where we have failed. Whether they are inspired by faith, life experiences, or compassion, we as Christians need to come alongside and help these heroes and good Samaritans because God uses everyone for His purpose. Remember—God does not need us to reach His purpose, but praise God, He allows us to help.

GREEN BERET
PROJECT

| **Building Strong Foundations Through Community Partnerships** |

Our Vision

That all youth in underserved communities throughout America will be given the opportunity to live flourishing lives of personal responsibility and leadership.

Our Mission

The Green Beret Project empowers youth through dynamic, community-based programs that foster leadership, academic success, critical thinking, and personal growth.

Building Leaders, One Community at a Time

Our Core Values

Youth Empowerment: Committed to empowering youth to become adult leaders through comprehensive support and mentorship.

Community Engagement: Engage with local communities to build strong, supportive networks that foster youth development and community improvement.

Holistic Development: We provide holistic support that addresses the academic, emotional, and socio-economic needs of our youth, ensuring their overall well-being and success.

Have questions or want to get involved with the Green Beret Project? Reach out to us! Whether you're looking to volunteer, donate, or learn more about our mission, we're here to help. Contact us today, and let's make a difference together.

Phone: (302)-602-9377

Email: info@greenberetproject.org

Website: Greenberetproject.org

STREET GRACE™

The sexual exploitation of children for commercial gain is one of the
greatest evils of our day. We're on a mission to end it.

HERE'S HOW...

Prevention
Preventing sexual exploitation by training parents, youth, and caring adults

Protection
Caring for at-risk children and survivors of sexual exploitation

Policy
Shaping legislation to reduce impunity for perpetrators and better care for survivors

Pursuit
Leveraging the power of AI to deter sexual predators online

As an organization led by a team of subject matter experts and guided by a council of
survivors, we're painfully aware of the devastation caused by the Commercial Sexual
Exploitation of Children. We won't rest until every child is protected and empowered.

JOIN US IN OUR WORK!

streetgrace.org
(678) 809-2111
info@streetgrace.org

Street Grace is a nonprofit organization that is eradicating the
sexual exploitation of children through prevention, protection,
policy, and pursuit.

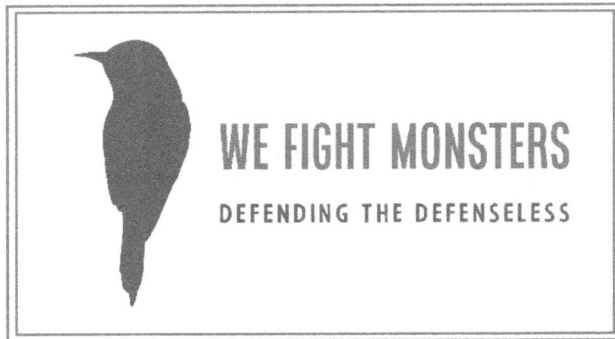

WE FIGHT MONSTERS

DEFENDING THE DEFENSELESS

We Fight Monsters is a beacon of hope in the darkest corners of our communities. Our mission is to confront and conquer the twin evils of human and narcotics trafficking, bringing light to places long shadowed by despair. We are a coalition of the brave – former special operators, law enforcement professionals, ex-cons, former gang members, and addiction recovery champions. United by a common goal, we venture into the most hostile areas to shut down sources of human suffering, rescue the exploited, and rehabilitate lives. By reclaiming neighborhoods, supporting victims, and empowering the vulnerable, we strive to lift communities from the depths of hopelessness to new heights of hope and dignity. Together, we fight not just monsters but for the chance of a brighter tomorrow for all.

Empowering Change: Our Impact by the Numbers

Every number tells a story of resilience, transformation, and hope. Here's the difference we've made together

250 People Recovered	75 People in Housing	4 Homeless Families Homed	4 Babies Born
Lives Reclaimed: Individuals Rescued from Despair	Safe Havens: Residents Now in Secure Housing	Families Restored: Homeless Households Given Shelte	New Beginnings: Infants Born Into Hope and Safety

About Us

Welcome to We Fight Monsters, where valor meets compassion in the heart of America's toughest battles against human and narcotics trafficking. Born from the gritty resolve of former special operators, law enforcement heroes, and courageous survivors, our foundation stands as a fortress against the darkest forces that prey upon the vulnerable. From the shadowed streets of urban despair to the hidden corners where exploitation thrives, we're not just a team; we're a movement. A movement fueled by unwavering commitment, hard-won expertise, and an unshakeable belief in second chances. Here, every action, every mission, every life touched, is a testament to our relentless pursuit of hope and healing. Dive into our story, witness our journey, and discover how, together, we're turning the tide against the monsters among us.

Contact us

Website: Wefightmonsters.org

Website: Flandersfields.org

Our Merchandise Stores

Onceamerican.com

Disciplesarmor.com

Chris Hennessy, along with Kara and Josh Henson (Chris's sister and brother-in-law), have come together with a shared mission rooted in faith and compassion.

Their guiding verse is Luke 12:24 (NLT):

"Look at the ravens. They don't plant or harvest or store food in barns, for God feeds them. And you are far more valuable to him than any birds!"

This mission was born out of personal tragedy. After losing their brother Eric to fentanyl poisoning—when he unknowingly purchased Adderall laced with fentanyl—they were compelled to take action.

Driven by a deep desire to make a difference, they are committed to combating drug abuse and human trafficking within their community and beyond, offering hope and support to those in need.

Contact us:

TheRavenisHere.org

theraven@theravenishere.org

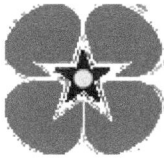

"Every hour that passes is another veteran that may be lost forever while in desperate need of help or support."

Our Mission

Flanders Fields mission is to set up as many Flanders-owned clean living facilities as possible, getting Vets clean and off the streets, and as part of 12-step recovery, we help those vets live out their 12th step ("Having had a spiritual awakening as the result of these Steps, we tried to carry this message to those still suffering, and to practice these principles in all our affairs") through our volunteer missions, both in the United States and around the world. We have found through experience that finding purpose is critical to long-term recovery, and for veterans in particular, continuing a life of service is mission-critical. We use Flanders Vets in recovery to tackle everything from conflict evacuation to human trafficking to homelessness to community revitalization.

Who We Are

Flanders Fields is a group of Army, Navy, Marine, and Air Force veterans on a mission to help other veterans in any way possible. As veterans, we understand the true problems and situations our soldiers deal with when coming home. Veterans are often faced with great challenges after service, including PTSD, TBI (Traumatic Brain Injury), alcoholism, overmedication, homelessness, and opiate addiction.

Please mail correspondence to:

P.O. Box 953

Cumming, GA 30028

WWW.Flandersfields.org

CALLED2DUTY
POWER-N-PURPOSE

STANDING TOGETHER. SAVING LIVES.

MISSION

Leveraging both our lived experience and that of those we serve, our mission is to **connect, empower, and educate** Service Members, Veterans, and their families (SMVF) through **prevention and recovery**. We achieve this by facilitating **training, comprehensive support, and increased access** to vital resources. Rooted in the **dimensions of wellness**, we are committed to building resilient, well-integrated communities where every individual can thrive.

VISION

We envision a future where Service Members, Veterans, and their families (SMVF) are supported by strong, inclusive networks that ensure their well-being and success. Called2Duty strives to be a leading force in fostering resilient, connected communities, exemplifying collaboration and innovation in all we do.

OUR PRIORITIES

◈ **Education** – Raising awareness and spreading **critical resources** about the **opioid crisis**.

◈ **Prevention** – Implementing **community-based strategies** that engage SMVF and local citizens to **reduce opioid dependency and its consequences**.

◈ **Safe Streets & Crime Prevention** – Empowering SMVF to lead **community safety initiatives**, reducing opioid-related crime.

◈ **Workforce Reintegration** – Helping **SMVF affected by the opioid crisis** reintegrate into the workforce, promoting **economic stability**.

◈ **Recovery Support** – Launching a **Veteran Peer Support National Pilot** to strengthen **long-term recovery** for SMVF.

◈ **Overdose Reduction** – **Training individuals** to recognize overdose signs and administer **Naloxone**, saving lives.

◈ **Maximizing State Resources** – Utilizing **existing state resources** to enhance **program effectiveness and sustainability**.

GET INVOLVED

♥ Donate – Your support helps us expand peer recovery programs, workforce reintegration, and Naloxone distribution.

♥ Volunteer – Help us train, educate, and support SMVF.

♥ Partner – Join forces with us to create lasting solutions for opioid prevention and recovery.

⚲ Visit Us: www.Called2Duty.com

✉ Contact: info@Called2Duty.com

Together, we can save lives and build stronger communities.

COVENANT RESCUE GROUP

Rescue. Redeem. Restore.

At Covenant Rescue Group, we believe in the biblical call to defend the defenseless and bring justice to the oppressed. Proverbs 31:8-9 commands us to "Speak up for those who cannot speak for themselves…defend the rights of the poor and needy." This is our mission. We exist to combat human trafficking and child exploitation, partnering with law enforcement to bring predators to justice and rescue the innocent from darkness.

Our Mission

We are a team of highly trained professionals—former military, law enforcement, and intelligence specialists—who dedicate our skills to identifying, disrupting, and dismantling human trafficking networks. Through direct operations, training law enforcement, and partnering with aftercare organizations, we ensure that survivors not only find freedom but also experience true restoration.

Why We Do This

Human trafficking is one of the greatest evils of our time, enslaving millions in unimaginable suffering. As followers of Christ, we cannot turn a blind eye. We are called to action, to be the hands and feet of Jesus in this battle. When we rescue a child from the grip of traffickers, we are not only saving a life—we are declaring God's love, justice, and redemption in a broken world.

If you want to learn more about our organization or if you want to donate, you can visit our website at **www.covenantrescue.org**

Human Trafficking and child exploitation are among the darkest evils our world has ever known.

CITY OF REFUGE

ABOUT CITY OF REFUGE

City of Refuge provides light, hope, and transformation for every individual we serve.

UNDERSTANDING THE NEED

City of Refuge is located in the middle of one of Atlanta's most historic and struggling neighborhoods where nearly 40% of the residents live below the Federal Poverty Level.

- 60% of all murders in metro Atlanta take place in the 30314 zip code
- 10% annual unemployment rate, compared to just 4% county-wide
- 26% violent crime rate, compared to 15% citywide
- 38% of residential units vacant, compared to 5% citywide
- Almost 65% of households are renting, and one-third of households now pay over 50% of their income in rent

OUR PROCESS

Our process takes place under one roof in the most dangerous zip code in Atlanta. The needs are great, but when like-minded community members, organizations, and volunteers partner together, we can see amazing things happen.

1. Get Stable
Housing, food, clothing, healthcare

2. Learn New Skills
Education, job training, financial literacy

3. Thrive In Community
New jobs, affordable housing, stronger families

OUR PROCESS AND PROGRAMS

Utilizing a one-stop shop approach, City of Refuge empowers individuals and families to overcome crisis, build momentum, and achieve their full potential.

LEARN MORE ABOUT OUR COMPREHENSIVE PROGRAMS

Job Training

We provide individuals with job training, mentorship, soft skills, and placement services, helping them build meaningful careers and a brighter future for their families.

Housing

We offer men, women, and children access to the highest quality temporary housing, along with a clear path to safe, permanent, and affordable housing, helping them regain stability and thrive.

JOB TRAINING

HOUSING

YOUTH DEVELOPMENT

HEALTH & WELLNESS

Youth Development

We offer year-round education, care, and enrichment for children from birth through 12th grade in a safe and nurturing environment where they can learn, grow, and succeed.

Health & Wellness

Our campus delivers a full spectrum of essential health services, addressing physical, mental, emotional, and spiritual well-being, empowering individuals to live balanced and healthy lives.

CAMPUS MAP

5 acres under one roof

- Housing
- Job Training
- Health & Wellness
- Youth Development

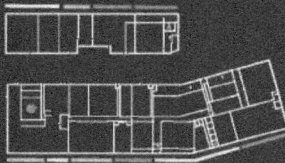

GET INVOLVED

CityofRefugeAtl.org

Take A Tour

Make A Donation

Serve With Us

1300 Joseph E. Boone Blvd NW, Atlanta, GA 30314

SOFM
SOFMISSIONS.ORG
EMPOWERING WARRIORS TO FIND PURPOSE & BE RESILIENT

BE RESILIENT CLINIC

HISTORY

Founded in 2011 by Dr. Damon Friedman, a 20-year special ops 100% service disabled combat veteran, and his wife Dayna. After overcoming the challenges of combat and military service, the Friedman's felt called to focus on combatting the suicide epidemic among the veteran community.

OUR SOLUTION

Providing restorative whole health care to veterans and military service members and putting them on a path to peak performance. The treatment model of our program, the Be Resilient Clinic, takes an intradisciplinary approach and addresses the areas of psychological, physical, spiritual, and social wellness. Veterans who apply and are accepted receive up to 365 days of care at no cost. This is made possible by our generous private donor base and state funding.

BE RESILIENT CLINICS

A 1-week intensive clinic that brings together providers from psychological, social, spiritual and physical domains to assess, treat and overcome challenges of military service and combat such as PTSD, chronic/acute pain, sleep, isolation, stress, and moral injury.

LIST OF PROVIDERS

- Physician
- Cognitive Therapist
- Physical Therapist
- Mental Health Counselor
- Nutritionist
- Strength and Conditioning Coach

- Chiropractor
- Acupuncturist
- Massage Therapist
- Recreational Therapist
- Spiritual Mentor
- Social Reintegration Therapist

📞 (813)-265-1711   📍 5121 EHRLICH RD STE 108, TAMPA, FL 33624   ✉ CONNECT@SOFMISSIONS.ORG

[SOF MISSIONS IMPACT]

50 STATES providing service across the nation

24 VA HOSPITALS serving chaplains and providers

400+ WARRIORS attended the Be Resilient Clinics

60 GROUPS empowered with Veteran Resources

3000 VETERANS received collaborative care and services

300,000 ATTENDEES at one hundred Speaking Engagements

[RESULTS]

Warriors suffering from moderate to extreme anxiety
73% Starting Program
12% Ending Program
VS

Warriors have strong negative beliefs about themselves, people and/or the world
61% Starting Program
11% Ending Program
VS

Warriors that feel distant or cut off from other people
77% Starting Program
22% Ending Program
VS

Warriors experiencing moderate to severe pain daily
65% Starting Program
25% Ending Program
VS

SOF MISSIONS IS A NONPROFIT 501(c)3 ORGANIZATION. SERVICES TO QUALIFYING VETERANS ARE PROVIDED FREE OF CHARGE.

SOF Missions addresses the suicide epidemic by delivering comprehensive, whole-health medical care to veterans and military service members. The organization's *Be Resilient Clinics* are one-week medical intensives designed to support up to 10 veterans with a multidisciplinary team of approximately 20 healthcare providers. These clinics take a holistic, intradisciplinary approach to treatment, focusing on psychological, physical, social, and spiritual well-being. Providers assess and address the unique challenges faced by military personnel, including PTSD, mild traumatic brain injury, chronic and acute pain, sleep disturbances, social isolation, stress, and moral injury. Following the clinic, veterans continue to receive ongoing care for up to one year, including follow-up appointments at 30, 60, and 90 days, as well as a six-month check-up with our medical team. All services are provided at no cost to the veterans.

About SOF Missions: https://vimeo.com/529316165

Be Resilient Clinic Video: https://vimeo.com/529337339

Phone: 813-265-2713

Website: www.sofmissions.org

Email: dayna@sofmissions.org

Address: 5121 Ehrlich Rd Ste. 108, Tampa, FL 33624

Modern Day Heroes

In our world, the word hero has taken on the meaning of heroic, herculean tasks done by superheroes who are superhuman. But in reality, true modern-day heroes may do heroic deeds that seem superhuman but are accomplished by our neighbors.

Most often, what makes them heroes is the willingness to step into the gap for the less fortunate, start a movement that solves a problem, or give a hand up that no one else was willing to give. The human spirit is an amazing, divinely inspired emotion that drives us to achieve success, win the contest, and want to be the best.

Although we all possess it in some form, there are those among us who personify the vitality and selflessness that only come when we embrace that spirit in all its divine intention and serve others and the greater good.

This section recognizes those who are doing just that. They have found places to serve outside or inside the nonprofit space, but nonetheless, they are doing great things for their fellow man.

Whether it is serving our veterans, fighting terrorism, rescuing the abused, or many other worthy causes, these are the leaders in our world who stepped up selflessly and attended to an inequity they saw. Whether they knew it or not, it was God-inspired and God infused.

These are the men and women who answered the call and deserve to be recognized outside of the organizations they founded or the cause they championed. These are not superheroes, just God's children who listened to the call and said, "If not me, who?"

Ben Owen

Ben is a daddy to eight (sometimes ten), grandparent to one, humanitarian, fighter of evil, bringer of hope, formerly addicted, alcoholic, and homeless. He's also the owner of BlackRifle Co, a data intelligence and digital media agency (not to be confused with the coffee company of a similar name) and co-founder of two non-profits—We Fight Monsters and Flanders Field—that help people in some of the worst places in America and the world. Ben loves sharing that his wife Jess can drive, load, and fire an M18 Hellcat, a WWII tank destroyer. He's also the only crackhead ever invited to

CIA headquarters. When they're not in South Memphis helping others rebuild their lives after addiction, Ben and Jess can be found in rural Georgia, where they live with their family.

Michael Dane Springer

Michael's commitment to helping others is deeply rooted in his experiences. His mission is to be the support and guidance he once needed, offering hope and assistance to those in similar circumstances. His dedication is evident through his volunteer work with the P.A.C.T. recovery program at the Lonoke County Sheriff's Office, where he actively contributes to the education, investigation, and rehabilitation efforts in the community. Michael expresses his gratitude to Sheriff John Staley for enabling him to be part of these critical initiatives.

In addition to his role at the Sheriff's Office, Michael is deeply involved in several organizations dedicated to veterans and recovery. He is the Lead Veteran Peer for *Called2Duty*, a veteran recovery program aimed at combating the opioid crisis among veterans and their families. Michael also serves as an overdose responder in Lonoke County and serves as the President of *We Are the 22*, a veteran suicide intervention organization.

Michael's leadership and dedication are reflected in his past positions within the Veterans of Foreign Wars (VFW). He has served as the Sergeant-at-Arms for the State of Arkansas VFW, the Senior Vice Commander of VFW Post 7769 in Beebe, AR, and the Senior Vice Commander for VFW District 5. Furthermore, he is an active member of the Central Arkansas Veteran Healthcare Services (CAVHS) Mental Health Executive Council, Federal Veterans Affairs (VA), working to improve mental health services for veterans.

Michael is passionate about mentoring individuals in recovery programs, such as the ***Pathway to Freedom*** program, by visiting prisons and sharing his journey and insights.

Michael also speaks with every graduating class for the at-risk youth at the Camp Robinson CSTP program. He resides in Cabot, Arkansas, with his supportive wife, Kim, and their four beloved dogs. Michael's story is one of resilience, transformation, and unwavering dedication to serving others, particularly those facing the challenges he once overcame.

Combat Veteran

Overcame a 16 ½ year addiction to methamphetamine, homelessness, and incarceration

7 years in faith & recovery

Kevin Metcalf

Kevin Metcalf worked in military, state, local, and federal law enforcement before becoming a prosecuting attorney. He founded the National Child Protection Task Force (NCPTF) and was a founding member of Raven. Kevin has built a global reputation for pioneering innovative methods that combine legal strategy, open-source intelligence (OSINT), geospatial mapping, dark web investigations, cryptocurrency tracing, and image analysis to assist law enforcement agencies around the world.

Through his leadership, Kevin has played a critical role in the recovery of countless missing and exploited children and the identification and apprehension of sexual predators across multiple countries. His unique ability to synthesize legal expertise with cutting-edge investigative technologies has positioned him as an

189

international leader in counter-human trafficking and child exploitation investigations. Kevin's mission-driven work continues to advance global collaboration, helping law enforcement and multidisciplinary teams disrupt trafficking networks and bring victims home.

Justin Downen

Justin Downen has lived a life of service and stands as a man, husband, father, veteran, and civil servant who goes above and beyond in all he does. His achievements go far beyond his resume, and as a friend of mine, I knew he needed recognition that he would never claim. His passion for the troubled youth in his area sets him apart as a hero. A man of faith and a brother in Christ, his counsel and friendship are priceless. His input and advice are always uplifting and infused with wisdom.

Justin Downen has served as an FBI Special Agent since 2011. During his time in the Bureau, he has investigated criminal and counterterrorism cases while also serving on the SWAT team, teaching firearms and active shooter response courses. He is currently the FBI liaison to large companies in Delaware and Maryland.

In 2017, Downen was profiled in the FBI's annual report because of his work on a 50-year-old cold case murder. His work as the case agent resulted in a successful prosecution, and it remains one of the oldest cold cases solved by the FBI. In 2019, Downen received the FBI Director's Award and the FBI William Webster Award for founding and leading the ***Green Beret Project***. The Green Beret Project is a non-profit organization that trains and mentors impoverished youth. By using methods made famous by Army Special Forces, the Green Beret Project is able to operate effective training programs in high-crime areas with limited resources. Prior to joining the FBI and 19th Special Forces Group in 2011, Downen was a member of 3rd Special Forces Group. Downen served in 3rd Special Forces Group from 2007-2011.

Downen has served in the military for 22 years. He joined the Missouri National Guard in 2000 and served there while earning a bachelor's degree from Southwest Baptist University. He now serves in the Delaware National Guard, where he trains and mentors new soldiers while also working with Special Forces National Guard recruiting to find and prepare the next generation of Green Berets. Downen has been married for 14 years and has three children. He gives all glory to God for anything he has accomplished while at the same time thanking the many talented professionals he has learned from over the years. He is especially thankful for the current and former members of 3rd Special Forces Group who led by example as they taught him the importance of creativity, hard work, humility, and servant leadership.

Bruce Deel

Bruce Deel is the Founder and CEO of City of Refuge, an Atlanta-based non-profit working to bring light, hope, and transformation to those living on the margins. The City of Refuge provides housing, education, medical, dental, vision, and mental health care, as well as vocational training for those leaving homelessness, returning from incarceration, or overcoming addiction. In addition, the City of Refuge offers an array of support services for survivors of domestic violence and sex trafficking, and Bruce founded MOST, Men Opposing Sex Trafficking, an organization supporting anti-trafficking efforts in 3 areas: Prevention, Interdiction, and Recovery.

Bruce is the author of Trust First and serves as a speaker and consultant to corporate and non-profit organizations around the country. He has been featured as a TEDx Speaker and is listed in the Guinness Book of World Records for participating in the Longest Consecutive Softball Game, 121 hours, which raised funds to fight sex trafficking. Bruce was named Alumnus of the Year for 2024 by his alma mater, Lee University.

He has been married to his wife, Rhonda, for 37 years and is the father of 5 beautiful daughters and Papa to 13 extraordinary grandchildren.

www.ingramcontent.com/pod-product-compliance
Lightning Source LLC
LaVergne TN
LVHW051230080426
835513LV00016B/1508